Smart Tourism Destination Governance

Drawing upon empirical research and critical literature review, *Smart Tourism Destination Governance: Technology and Design-Based Approach* provides a comprehensive overview and analysis of smart tourism destination governance and its related challenges.

Building on the author's extensive research background in tourism destinations and information technologies, the book provides a quantitative approach to the phenomenon, using cluster and network analysis. It uses design thinking to provide solutions on how to overcome the challenges faced within the context of tourism destination governance, with a detailed discussion of the contribution of the smart approach to overcoming such challenges. The book is presented in three parts as follows:

Part 1: The Need for a New Form of Tourism Destination Governance
Part 2: The Contribution of Smart Approach to Overcoming the Challenges of Tourism Destination Governance
Part 3: Designing Smart Tourism Destination Governance Towards Sustainability, Competitiveness and Resilience

This work will be of great interest to both tourism scholars and decision-makers within the field of tourism, aiming to provide a detailed overview of and broaden the reader's horizons in regards to the possibilities of the smart approach to tourism destination governance.

Tomáš Gajdošík is an associate professor at the Department of Tourism, Faculty of Economics, Matej Bel University in Banská Bystrica, Slovakia. In his research, he focuses on smart tourism and tourism information technologies. He also deals with the issues of destination management, governance and leadership. To date, he has contributed to several monographs, textbooks and scientific journals.

Routledge Focus on Tourism and Hospitality

Routledge Focus on Tourism and Hospitality presents small books on big topics and how they intersect with the world of tourism and hospitality research. The idea is to fill the gap between journal articles and books. This new short-form series offers both established and early-career academics the flexibility to publish cutting-edge commentary on key areas of tourism and hospitality, topical issues, policy-focused research, analytical or theoretical innovations, a summary of the key players or short topics for specialized audiences in a succinct way.

World Heritage and Tourism
Marketing and Management
Bailey Ashton Adie

Tourism and Urban Regeneration
Processes Compressed in Time and Space
Alberto Amore

Tourism, Sanctions and Boycotts
Siamak Seyfi and C. Michael Hall

Mountaineering Tourism
A Critical Perspective
Michal Apollo and Yana Wengel

Managing People in Commercial Kitchens
A Contemporary Approach
Charalampos Giousmpasoglou, Evangelia Marinakou, Anastasios Zopiatis and John Cooper

Smart Tourism Destination Governance
Technology and Design-Based Approach
Tomáš Gajdošík

For more information about this series, please visit: https://www.routledge.com/tourism/series/FTH

Smart Tourism Destination Governance

Technology and Design-Based Approach

Tomáš Gajdošík

Routledge
Taylor & Francis Group

LONDON AND NEW YORK

First published 2022
by Routledge
2 Park Square, Milton Park, Abingdon, Oxon OX14 4RN

and by Routledge
605 Third Avenue, New York, NY 10158

*Routledge is an imprint of the Taylor & Francis Group, an informa
business*

© 2022 Tomáš Gajdošík

The right of Tomáš Gajdošík to be identified as author of this work
has been asserted by him in accordance with sections 77 and 78 of
the Copyright, Designs and Patents Act 1988.

British Library Cataloguing-in-Publication Data
A catalogue record for this book is available from the British
Library

Library of Congress Cataloging-in-Publication Data
A catalog record has been requested for this book

ISBN: 978-1-032-21636-2 (hbk)
ISBN: 978-1-032-21637-9 (pbk)
ISBN: 978-1-003-26934-2 (ebk)

DOI: 10.4324/9781003269342

Typeset in Times New Roman
by SPi Technologies India Pvt Ltd (Straive)

Contents

Figures

Tables

Acknowledgements

The research was supported by the research project VEGA 1/0237/20 Tourism 4.0: Smart and sustainable tourism development in a competitive environment.

Abbreviations

3D	three-dimensional
AI	artificial intelligence
API	application programming interface
ARIMA	autoregressive integrated moving average
ATM	automated teller machine
BLE	Bluetooth low energy
CEE	Central and Eastern Europe
CRM	customer relationship management
DBSCAN	density-based spatial clustering of applications with noise
DMO	destination management organisation
DMS	destination management system
GIS	geographic information system
GPS	global positioning system
GPX	global positioning system exchange format
GSM	global system for mobile communication
HTML	hypertext mark-up language
HVG	horizontal visibility graph
ICT	information and communication technology
ID	identification
IDS	Internet distribution system
IP	Internet protocol
MDS	multi-dimensional scaling
NFC	near field communication
OTA	online travel agency
POS	point of sale
RFID	radio frequency identification
TMR	Tatry Mountain Resort
UGC	user-generated content
URL	uniform resource locator
WOM	word of mouth

Introduction

The word 'smart' has become a buzzword not only in the academic sphere but also in the practice. Almost everything is becoming smart. People use smartphones, construct smart buildings and live in smart homes with smart TVs, smart refrigerators or smart heating. The smart concept has emerged as a result of the rise of information technology and the need for sustainability. Developments in technology, climate change and growing uncertainty stimulate the need to adapt to a very-fast-changing environment. Smart tourism describes the current stage of tourism development and how it is becoming a promising way to face these new market conditions.

Smart tourism is considered as a future of tourism that revolutionises the way how technologies, innovation and cooperation are used to better design tourist experience, stimulate wellbeing of residents, enhance competitiveness of businesses and destinations. Many destinations around the world started to adopt the smart approach due to its ability to deal with mass tourism and over tourism-related issues. This approach is built on information and communication technologies (ICTs), advanced data analytics and design thinking that help to make right and timely decisions.

Different development policies were applied in different geographical regions. In Europe, the supranational policy based on the Strategy Europe 2020 for smart, sustainable and inclusive growth led to the support of the European Capital of Smart Tourism initiative, stimulating tourism destinations to adopt smart principles. Moreover, the national policy in Spain supports the development of smart tourism destinations through projects on local scale, coordinated by the Spanish National Society for Innovation and Tourism Technology Management (Segittur). Slovenian national tourism organisation supports smart destination branding aimed at enhancing experience and attracting

DOI: 10.4324/9781003269342-1

those tourists who love and appreciate natural and cultural attractions. In Asia, the pioneers of smart destination development were China and South Korea, where development policies were aimed mainly at supporting technical infrastructure and destination marketing. The current Australian tourism policy pays more attention to smart governance and the use of open data (Baggio, Micera & Del Chiappa, 2020). On the other hand, developing countries in Africa and South America focus more on barriers to smart tourism destination development. However, the current pandemic situation pushes forward policies focusing on building more resilient destinations (Gretzel 2021). For example, the European Union strategy for sustainable tourism adopted in 2021 focuses on the transition to sustainable, responsible and smart tourism and stresses the need to build destinations that are more resilient.

The challenge of smart tourism destinations lies more in governance than in technology, highlighting key aspects for the redesign of the functions of destination management organisations (Ivars-Baidal et al. 2019) leading to sustainable, competitive and resilient tourism destinations. Smart governance can be viewed as a tool to prepare the system to face the complex challenges attached to the pursuit of competitiveness and sustainability in a dynamic environment (Antonelli & Cappiello 2016), where complex sets of issues cannot be solved through linear rationalising and design thinking is welcomed (Crowley & Head 2017). However, little is known about how destination governance can be built according to smart principles (Errichiello & Micera 2021). Although there have been several attempts that conceptually address the ability of smart destination governance to support sustainability, competitiveness and resilience, so far this problematic lacks comprehensive empirical research.

As there is a scarcity of such research, tourism scholars are invited to contribute to building the theory and tools which can be used to better design, create and govern tourism places (Xiang et al. 2021). This book answers these calls and aims to provide the conceptual foundations of smart destination governance and its challenges, empirically analyse the contribution of smart approach to overcoming the identified challenges and design new perspectives for smart tourism destination governance focusing on sustainability, competitiveness and resilience. It builds on the author's more than 10-year research of tourism destinations and information technologies, as well as close cooperation with representatives of several tourism destinations. Slovakia is chosen as a reference country for the research, as the gradual development of tourism destination governance since the adoption of the market economy and the recognition of the country as a digital challenger make it an ideal 'living laboratory' for the phenomenon of smart destination governance.

References

Antonelli, G., and Cappiello, G., 2016. *Smart development in smart communities*. Oxfordshire: Taylor & Francis Group.

Baggio, R., Micera, R., and Del Chiappa, G., 2020. Smart tourism destinations: A critical reflection. *Journal of Hospitality and Tourism Technology*, 11 (3), 407–423.

Crowley, K., and Head, B.W., 2017. The enduring challenge of 'wicked problems': Revisiting Rittel and Webber. *Policy Sciences*, 50 (4), 539–547.

Errichiello, L., and Micera, R., 2021. A process-based perspective of smart tourism destination governance. *European Journal of Tourism Research*, 29 (2021).

Gretzel, U., 2021. Smart toursim development. *In:* P. Dieke, B. King, and R. Sharpley, eds. *Tourism in development*. Oxford: CABI, 159–168.

Ivars-Baidal, J.A., Celdrán-Bernabeu, M.A., Mazón, J.N., and Perles-Ivars, Á.F., 2019. Smart destinations and the evolution of ICTs: A new scenario for destination management? *Current Issues in Tourism*, 22 (13), 1581–1600.

Xiang, Z., Stienmetz, J., and Fesenmaier, D.R., 2021. Smart tourism design: Launching the annals of tourism research curated collection on designing tourism places. *Annals of Tourism Research*, 86, 103154.

Part 1

The need for a new form of tourism destination governance

Tourism destinations are the *raison d'être* of tourism and its development. They are the key element of the tourism system and places of interaction among various stakeholders activated by tourists. In order to be competitive, sustainable and resilient, tourism destinations need to have rules and mechanisms for steering destination development and enabling effective decision-making. Therefore, tourism destination governance is needed. Today's tourism destination governance is confronted with a highly complex and dynamic environment, creating several challenges that are hard to solve through linear rationalising. Developments in technology, climate change and growing uncertainty are altering common governance models and make it increasingly difficult to steer the destination development in such a complex socio-technical system (Volgger et al. 2021). The interaction between a destination, its stakeholders and tourists is changing towards user-centeredness, while a more collaborative approach is needed. Information and communication technologies (ICTs) can foster the experience co-creation and facilitate decision-making (Buhalis et al. 2019). Within the complex sets of issues, traditional approaches to destination governance have reached their limits and a new form of governance is being sought.

To achieve better governance, technological solutions applied to the growing amount of data available can bring new knowledge to destinations. With the help of the design approach, this part of the book provides the conceptual foundations of smart destination governance. Based on an in-depth literature review, the foundations of destination governance and its challenges are outlined. Moreover, it deals with the fact that a complex and changing environment forces the implementation of a smart concept with design thinking to destination governance. Although the importance of using design thinking in destination development was established almost 50 years ago (Gunn 1972), the

DOI: 10.4324/9781003269342-2

recent advances in information technologies make it possible to overcome the limitations of previous methods and provide a more analytical approach to this phenomenon. This situation pushes forward the concept of smart tourism destination governance, which integrates the use of ICTs and design principles in decision-making and steering the destination development. Smart destination governance is built on transdisciplinary thinking, taking into account addressing complex issues in a human-centred and participatory manner. With the help of technologies and data analytics, it supports the tourist-centric approach, underpinned by design thinking methodology, and focuses on experience enrichment. Moreover, it builds on public policy approach to decision-making, based on the need for collaboration between the main stakeholders through the use of technologies, which is evident mainly in the smart city concept.

References

Buhalis, D., Harwood, T., Bogicevic, V., Viglia, G., Beldona, S., and Hofacker, C., 2019. Technological disruptions in services: Lessons from tourism and hospitality. *Journal of Service Management*, 30 (4), 484–506.
Gunn, C., 1972. *Vacationscape: Designing tourist areas.* Austin: Bureau of Business Research, University of Texas at Austin.
Volgger, M., Erschbamer, G., and Pechlaner, H., 2021. Destination design: New perspectives for tourism destination development. *Journal of Destination Marketing & Management*, 19 (March), 100561.

1 Tourism destination governance and its challenges

Tourism destinations are focal points of tourism activity and an important subject of tourism research. They are the fundamental unit of analysis in any modelling of a tourism system (Pike 2008). Although there are several ways to define tourism destination, the current research streams highlight mainly the fact that tourism destination consists of a number of different components. From the supply-side perspective, there are stakeholders of different sizes and structures. Tourists and their behaviour represent the demand side. There are dynamic connections among these components, which are many times non-linear, resulting from the fact that there are rarely simple cause and effect relationships between these elements and a small stimulus may cause a large effect, or no effect at all (e.g. the law of diminishing returns in economics). Moreover, due to the impact of the external environment, these relations are open and unpredictable (Baggio 2008). From this point of view, tourism destinations are viewed as complex adaptive systems of interrelated and independent stakeholders (Baggio 2008; Pearce 2014), where the tourism demand meets the supply.

Even if it was not explicitly defined as such, the idea that tourism is a complex system has been discussed for a long time. The European, mainly German-speaking, economic literature is much aware of Kaspar's model of tourism system (Kaspar 1976). It consists of two subsystems – subject and object that are under the impact of economic, social, ecological, political and technological spheres. The Anglo-Saxon literature focusing on tourism geography was influenced by the Leiper's system model of tourism (Leiper 1979). It comprises two subsystems (components) – tourist generating regions and tourist destinations connected by transit routes and influenced by broader environments: physical, cultural, social, economic, political and technological. These models helped to understand the structure and

DOI: 10.4324/9781003269342-3

dynamic evolutions of the tourism system. In this system, tourist behaviour, measured as both spatial and temporal flows, activates the production system of tourism experiences and the supply of tourism products within a destination (Choe & Fesenmaier 2021). Therefore, tourism destinations are increasingly viewed as experience production systems (Tussyadiah 2014). This complexity makes destinations difficult to manage in terms of sustainability, competitiveness and resilience.

1.1 Approaches to tourism destination development

To understand and promote the sustainable competitiveness of tourism destination and its development, several approaches have been developed by tourism researchers (Pechlaner, Kozak, & Volgger 2014). The most discussed ones include destination management, governance and leadership. The debate on destination management has evolved mainly alongside two streams of research. The first focused on destination marketing (e.g. Pike 2008; Pike & Page 2014), while the latter gave attention to the much broader management concept related to strategising, exercising control, coordinating organisations and leveraging destination resources (Hristov & Zehrer 2015) towards competitiveness. Destination management has been a primary concern with defining objectives and trying to achieve these mechanisms by corporate thinking with a special focus on relatively broad authority of destination management organisations (DMOs) (Pechlaner, Beritelli, Pichler, Peters, & Scott 2015). The management concept puts forward managerial understanding relying on the hierarchical nature of bureaucratic structure (Bramwell & Lane 2011). This conventional top-down approach has not fully taken into consideration the need for stakeholder participation in the destination development.

Many scholars (e.g. Beritelli & Bieger 2014; Hall 2008) understate this top-down, centralised and bureaucratic approach of the public sector, and provide recommendations to an alternative 'bottom-up', decentralised form of governance in which stakeholders, together with local communities, are determined to take more responsibility for destination management, marketing and planning of collaborative actions. Therefore, academics and practitioners started to focus more on highlighting multi-actor complexity, public–private interdependency, coordination, control and leadership. This shift to a more bottom-up approach, where businesses and local communities were encouraged to provide input to destination development has been observed (Vernon et al. 2005). This led to a change in the perspective towards destination governance focused on processes and structures. As a complement to destination governance, destination leadership is being discussed, dealing with the role of leaders and how they influence other stakeholders (Pechlaner et al. 2014). This sound approach has been gaining more and more attention as destinations are highly fragmented and involve a diverse set of stakeholders having contrasting objectives and divergent priorities (Hristov & Zehrer 2015). Looking at destination leadership as a supplemental dimension of destination governance, it can be concluded that destination governance is based on the common vision of tourism development, suitable organisational structures and instruments for decision-making and leaders who are able to lead stakeholders and motivate them in their common efforts (Kučerová et al. 2018).

The discussed approaches to tourism destination development have made significant contributions to the advancement of tourism destination research. However, as Volgger, Erschbamer and Pechlaner (2021) emphasise, these paradigms also suffer from shortcomings resulting from the concentration on more short- and medium-term impacts and partial disconnection of organisational and strategic consideration with the tourist experience. Therefore, destination governance should take more into account the interplay of supply-side dynamics and demand-based tourism experience. In this way, recent advancements in tourism design (Xiang & Fesenmaier 2017a) and destination design (Scuttari et al. 2021) can enrich the concept of tourism destination governance.

1.2 Foundations of tourism destination governance

The concept of governance was born centuries ago, but only in the 1990s it has begun to be used in tourism as well as in other fields, with much of the knowledge taking shape a decade later (Fayos-Solà 2016). In 1992, the use of the word 'governance' experienced a wide success with the publication of the World Bank report 'Governance and Development' stimulating the use of the expression 'from government to governance' (Plattner 2013). The term 'governance' derives from the word 'government'. Although they are sometimes treated as synonyms, a certain distinction should be made between them. A starting point is that the notion of governance is characterised by the idea of complexity and by the way in which power is exercised. In terms of government, the exercise of power takes the form of mere control and enforcement of the rules. In the concept of governance, societal development is central (Antonelli & De Liso 2016). Therefore, governance can be seen as an act of governing. In this sense, Hall (2011) identified six characteristic elements of governance models including participation and power sharing; multi-level integration; diversity and decentralisation; deliberation; flexibility and revisability; experimentation and knowledge sharing. Moreover, it can be stated that governance emphasises collaboration of the government with the private and civil society sectors, integration of organisations within government, use of new information technologies and attention to citizens' demands (Fayos-Solà 2016).

Based on the concept of governance in public policy and political science, Hall (2011) created a typology for governance and its implications for tourism policy analysis. Taking into account the relationships between public and private policy actors and the steering modes that range from hierarchical steering to non-hierarchical approaches, four different modes of tourism governance were outlined. *Hierarchical* governance is conducted through vertically integrated state structures, while the use of *markets* as governance mechanisms moves to the directions of self-regulation. Network governance is seen as a middle way between hierarchical and market governance and is characterised by interdependence, resource exchange and significant autonomy from the state (Rhodes 2007). The fourth approach to governance is *communities*, which highlights the importance of public participation in policy-making (Piere & Peters 2020).

The concept of governance applied to tourism destination has started to be broadly discussed since 2007, with the conceptual paper of Beritelli, Bieger, and Laesser (2007). The authors claim that destination governance consists of setting and developing rules and mechanisms for a policy, as well as business strategies, by involving all the institutions and individuals. Destination governance focuses on the role of influential actors, their interests, affiliations and the roles they play in destination development (Beritelli & Bieger 2014).

From a normative manner, destination governance demands destination managers to explicitly consider the blurred nature of tourism destinations to guarantee, among others, a responsible, accountable, sustainable, efficient and effective coordination (Volgger et al. 2017). In this sense, destination governance should take into account the good governance principles. Ruhanen et al. (2010) conducted a systematic review of the literature dealing with political governance and business governance issues. Although this review did not focus on tourism destination governance, the principles described by these authors could also be implemented in destination governance. Moreover, OECD (2012), as well as Hemmati, Dodds, Enayati, and McHarry

(2012), contributed to the research of good governance principles. Shields, Moore, and Eagles (2016) have taken over the characteristics of good governance identified by the United Nations Development Programme (UNDP 1997) and used them as ten principles of good governance of protected areas. Morrison (2019) used the six most frequent dimensions of good governance to evaluate destination governance (Table 1.1). Following these approaches, the concept of destination governance advocates for the need for socially responsible behaviour in tourism destinations (Gajdošík 2015a).

Due to the spatial connotations of destinations, destination governance is embedded into regional governance. Regional governance is an appropriate approach for coordinating and controlling regional integrated processes while concentrating on the ability to self-organise and control regional structures. However, as DMOs play a crucial role in the governance of tourism destinations, it is imperative to also consider corporate governance, which enhances business management, including the organisation of a company's top management to create a balance between competency, control and responsibility (Pechlaner, Volgger, & Herntrei 2012). In this sense, destination governance is seen as an interface between regional and corporate governance. Therefore, theories of corporate governance, which are relevant for businesses, but also theories of governance, which are relevant for national and/or

Table 1.1 Review of good governance principles

Ruhanen et al. (2010)	OECD (2012)	Hemmati et al. (2012)	Shields et al. (2016)	Morrison (2019)
Accountability	Accountability	Accountability	Accountability	Accountability
Transparency	Transparency	Transparency	Transparency	Transparency
Involvement	Effectiveness and efficiency	Effectiveness and efficiency	Effectiveness	Involvement
Structure	Responsiveness	Responsiveness	Efficiency	Structure
Effectiveness	Forward looking vision	Set of rules	Responsiveness	Effectiveness
Power	Rule of law	Stakeholders' participation	Strategic vision	Power
Efficiency	Legitimacy		Rule of law	
(De)centralisation	Inclusiveness		Public participation	
Shareholders rights	Integration		Consensus orientation	
Knowledge management	Capacity		Equity	
Legitimacy				

regional systems, should be applied to explain governance in a destination context (Table 1.2).

Property rights theory, transaction cost theory and resource dependency theory focus on the dyadic perspective of relationships between two companies or relationships between two interest groups within one company (Gulati 1998). Political theory focuses on assessing the

Table 1.2 Theories explaining governance in a destination context

Theory	Authors	Conception	Destination Context
Property rights theory	Coase (1960)	Focus on the allocation of property rights, behaviour of individuals, distributional conflicts	Distribution of property rights have an influence on the distribution and utilisation of destination resources
Transaction cost theory	Williamson (1975)	Focus on the costs organisations have to face as they undertake market transactions with other organisations	The level of transaction cost will determine whether new stakeholders will wish to enter collaborative partnerships
Political theory	Keohane and Nye (1977)	Focus on the disposition of power in society	Analysis of the power dynamics and the distribution of benefits among the participants of a collaborative agreement
Resource dependency theory	Pfeffer and Salancik (1978)	Focus on the explanation why individuals and organisations rely upon one other	Stakeholders use power-conflict assessment to determine whether they should compete or collaborate
Collaboration theory	Axelrod (1984)	Focus on the conditions under which the cooperation emerge	Cooperation enables destination stakeholders to gather the resources and achieve a synergic effect
Social network theory	Burt (1992)	Focus on the examination of complexity relationships between individuals, groups and organisations	Destination success is based on the formation of networks of destination stakeholders

Source: Elaborated based on Fyall, Garrod, and Wang (2012).

balance of power between states, organisations and individuals (Fyall et al. 2012), while the collaboration theory in the destination context is focused more on different ways of formalisation ranging from informal verbal agreements to legally binding agreements (Wood & Gray 1991). However, Beritelli et al. (2007) emphasise that in order to analyse the governance in a community-type destination and explain the underlying mechanisms, there is a need to take not only the dyadic perspective, but also the network perspective. Moreover, theories considering corporate governance provide a valuable starting point for destination governance; however, in the context of destinations, informal mechanisms, trust and knowledge are more important than in companies. Volgger, Pechlaner, and Pichler (2017) conclude that common to the publications concerned with destination governance classification is the character of the underlying dimensions that is strongly related to the network structure of destinations. The network perspective is important due to the fact that destination managers have limited coercive power over the stakeholders in a destination and in such situations, gaining competitive advantage should be based on the formation of networks consisting of less formalised relationships based on trust, reciprocity and inclusive governance (van der Zee et al. 2017).

1.3 Network governance of tourism destinations

The complexity and limited power of influencing the number of stakeholders resulted in a network approach to tourism destination and its governance (van der Zee et al. 2017, Valeri & Baggio 2020a). Network forms of governance are considered more flexible, with the potential to respond quickly to changes in their environment (Palmer 1998). The network governance occurs through social structures, characterised by a sense of common purpose and interests (Baggio et al. 2010). As a complement to network governance, network leadership implies the particular challenges of leading, organising and communicating with individual stakeholders and with destination network (Beritelli 2011; d'Angella & Go 2009; Kozak, Volgger, & Pechlaner 2014). Leadership networks in tourism destinations connect leaders who share common interests and who have a commitment to influence a field of practice or policy. Such networks make it easier for leaders to find common ground around the issues they care about, mobilise support, influence policy and the allocation of resources (Hoppe & Reinelt 2010). These approaches are considered as a tool for strengthening the sustainable competitiveness of destinations (Van der Zee

& Vanneste 2015), fostering innovation (Gajdošík, Gajdošíková, Maráková, & Borseková 2017), knowledge sharing (Raisi et al. 2020) and supporting resilience (Zehrer & Raich 2010). Moreover, promoting the network capability of a DMO increases its authority and thus the ability to govern the destination (Volgger & Pechlaner 2014). In the sense of network governance, destination is seen as a cluster of interrelated stakeholders embedded in a social network (Scott, Cooper, et al. 2008). In order to be effective, efficient, sustainable, legitimate and accepted, network coordination should take the form of stakeholder-oriented and collaborative governance rather than top-down management (Volgger & Pechlaner 2015). By means of synergic activities of planning and organisation, the strength of such a network can be enhanced to the advantage of any single stakeholder (Valeri and Baggio 2020b). The networks in a destination can be classified based on several criteria (Table 1.3).

The network membership is based on the classification of supply-side and demand-side stakeholders. In the supply-side networks, separate networks of tourism service providers, intermediaries or tourism associations can be taken into account creating sub-networks (Cehan et al. 2021) or overall inter-organisational networks of tourism stakeholders can be found (Gajdošík 2015b). Furthermore, stakeholders from other industries related to tourism can be included in the destination network (Presenza & Cipollina 2010). Demand-side networks include tourists and their flows within and outside of destinations (Beritelli, Reinhold, & Laesser 2020).

In terms of geographical distribution, the networks are classified as local, regional or national. While local destination networks focus more on community and/or commercial interests (Gibson et al. 2005), the regional networks can have vertical collaboration gaps related to

Table 1.3 Classification of networks in tourism destinations

Criteria	Description
Network membership	supply side, demand side
Geographical distribution	local, regional, national
Nature of linkages	formal vs. informal
Type of network	real vs. virtual
Type of exchange	cooperation, leadership, knowledge, mobility
Network morphology	cohesion, centrality, clustering, efficiency

Source: Elaborated based on Baggio et al. (2010); Shaw and Conway (2000); Sørensen and Balsby (2020).

the scale of network-building (Stoddart et al. 2020) and can access intra-destination linkages (Michálková 2011). National networks are mostly horizontal networks created by associations (e.g. hospitality or travel agency associations) (Magaš & Meler 2013).

As a result of a collaborative approach among stakeholders in a tourism destination, formal and informal networks are being created. Formal networks are institutionalised relationships among existing stakeholders. They are networks where the process of joint decision-making involving key stakeholders, aiming at avoiding or resolving conflicts by advancing shared visions and goals takes place (Gray 1989; Jamal & Getz 1995; Hall 1999). It can be done by establishing DMOs or other legally binding forms of collaboration. Informal networks are based on good and productive relations between network members without creating a formal organisation (Gajdošík, Gajdošíková, Maráková, & Borseková 2017).

Although the majority of research on destination networks have been done using real networks, Baggio and Del Chiappa (2014) tried to analyse virtual networks created based on hyperlinks among stakeholders' websites in three destinations – Elba, Gallura, Livigno. Further, Del Chiappa and Baggio (2015) confirm that a strong structural cohesion exists between the real and the virtual components (websites). This leads to the fact that the smart digital ecosystem needs to be fully considered when dealing with tourism activities at a destination (Baggio 2017).

Destination network ties can be created based on certain attributes. The most common is cooperation in product development or marketing communication (Gajdošík 2015b), strategy and policy design, supply of goods and services or accessing funds (Cehan et al. 2021). Power and its exercise can be another attribute (Gajdošík, Gajdošíková, Maráková, & Flagestad 2017) that affects destination governance and leadership. Destination leaders are those tourism stakeholders that are powerful enough to lead tourism development (Tuohino & Konu 2014). These leaders provide strategic direction to destinations; however, they need resources and power (Pechlaner, Herntrei, Pichler, & Volgger 2012). Tourism destinations have to be innovative to maintain competitiveness; therefore, effective knowledge transfer in a destination network is the prerequisite for innovation (Raisi et al. 2020). Demand-oriented networks deal mainly with mobility issues of tourists (Asero et al. 2016). Tourists not only flow through the physical space of a destination, but virtual flows between the Internet pages can be observed as the trip experience phases are influenced by information technologies (Laesser et al. 2019).

Concerning the methodological perspective, techniques and analytic methods of complex networks provide several opportunities to analyse network topology (Valeri & Baggio 2020b). Network science is focused on enumerating, mapping and analysing the patterns of connections between elements of a system (Baggio 2017). Network techniques are fundamentally based on the mathematical techniques of graph theory. A network is represented by a graph and/or an adjacency matrix. The identification between a graph and matrix enables to use methods of linear algebra to analyse the network characteristics. As tourism destination is a prototypical complex phenomenon and understanding of stakeholder relations is of crucial importance, network science is the most powerful approach for investigating the structure of a destination. From an applied perspective, network analysis provides the baseline needed to design and govern destinations, as they need to be grounded in a deep knowledge of the system's features (Baggio 2020).

Although tourism destinations are ideal object of study of network science, this method has been neglected for a long time by tourism researchers (Baggio 2017). At the beginning of the 21st century, tourism scholars started to elaborate on the idea of a network approach. The first studies of networks in tourism were mostly qualitative, dealing with aggregated or dyadic relationships. Selin and Beason (1991) analysed inter-organisational relationships in tourism through the lenses of sociology and management. Palmer (1996) examined the building of networks by public and private tourism sector organisations. A more quantitative examination of destination networks started in the mid-2000s, focusing mainly on the supply-side networks. Scott, Baggio, and Cooper (2008) dealt with the structural properties of inter-organisational networks within destinations, while Presenza and Cipollina (2010) analysed the variety of relations existing in tourism networks, identified as complex and mutable entities, where a vast range of stakeholders coexist. Baggio, Scott, and Cooper (2010) reviewed the methods of networks science with the application to the field of tourism studies. Moreover, Beritelli, Strobl, and Peters (2013) focused on the networks of interlocks between local and non-local (outside the region, outside the country) board of directors for a set of salient organisations in six tourism destinations in Austria and Switzerland. The research of Del Chiappa and Presenza (2013) was aimed at using the network analysis to investigate a relationship and structural perspective to assess relationships among stakeholders in Italy. Grama and Baggio (2014) proposed insights on network science from a theoretical and practical point of view so that it can better inform governance policies in complex dynamic environments. Baggio, Scott, and Cooper (2013) have looked at network analysis as a useful tool in analysing policy development and improving inter-organisational network effectiveness. Ness, Aarstad, Haugland, and Gronseth (2014) applied network theory to explore how destination players search and make use of bridge ties to achieve knowledge transfer and destination development. Del Chiappa and Baggio (2015) used real and virtual components in the destinations' digital ecosystems. Gajdošík et al. (2017) examine the destination structure by identifying leaders in two mature mountain destinations. Czernek-Marszałek (2018) evaluated cooperation in a destination with the use of network analysis. Buffa, Beritelli, and Martini (2019) focused on project networks of actors involved in innovative products and reputation networks of salient actors for destinations' development. The most recent studies from Baggio (2020) and Raisi et al. (2020) focus on examining the structure of tourism destinations and knowledge transfer, respectively.

The demand perspective has not gained so much scientific attention. Shih (2006) analysed the network formed by drive tourism, while D'Agata, Gozzo, and Tomaselli (2013) mapped the spatial distribution of tourism mobility. Asero et al. (2016) analysed destination networks built through tourist mobility. Baggio and Scaglione (2018) used network analysis to identify strategic visitor flows.

Looking at topological characteristics used in supply- and demand-side networks in these works, the applicability of network metrics to help to improve network governance of tourism destinations can be summarised. Most of the initial applications concern the topological characterisation of destination networks and their peculiarities. These studies examine mainly the distribution of relationships in the network from the macroscopic – global – perspective (e.g. dealing with network density). Further, the networks of stakeholders started to be analysed using a microscopic perspective, focusing on the identification of the most relevant actors (using centrality measures) and analysing the innovation potential and knowledge transfer in destinations (focusing on efficiency) (Table 1.4).

Although the shift in the methodology from purely qualitative to more quantitative is evident in the presented research on destination networks and their governance, without a more in-depth knowledge of destination and its characteristics, it is not recommended to form definitive conclusions. In addition to this, Valeri and Baggio (2020b) propose modelling the dynamics of tourism destination phenomenon, as it can be seen as a tool for supporting the analysis and planning of

Table 1.4 Network analysis metrics useful for network governance of tourism destinations

Type of Exchange	Network Metrics
Cooperation	density, clustering coefficient, modularity
Leadership	centrality (degree, closeness, betweenness),
Knowledge transfer	local and global efficiency
Tourist mobility	centrality (in-degree, out-degree, betweenness), connected components, cliques

complex systems. Such a modelling can use simulations of knowledge diffusion or information spreading. Together, structural and dynamic characteristics of a destination are important to the governance of the destination, as well as its strategies, policies and activities. For a complex destination system, network science has proved to be a useful tool for describing complex associations in a tourism destination and has enabled tourism researchers to uncover details that would not have been easily recognisable (Baggio 2020). Although the presented studies show that the methods of network science are able to provide interesting and useful outcomes for theory and practice, their scarcity has brought a rather fragmented contribution to tourism destination research.

Although the theory stresses that the network approach to tourism governance could increase the capacity of a destination to adapt to changing circumstances and become more resilient (Zehrer & Raich 2010), van der Zee et al. (2017) indicate that limited formal power and dependency on external parties impedes the position of network managers. This indicates that network governance of destinations faces several challenges.

1.4 Challenges of tourism destination governance

The fast-changing environment, fuelled by developments in technology, climate change and recent crisis, puts another pressure on tourism destinations' development (Fyall & Garrod 2020). These disruptors change the behaviour of tourists (Pearce 2019), increase competition (Pike & Page 2014) and call for destination flexibility and resilience (Pechlaner & Innerhofer 2018). In order to identify the challenges of destination governance, a content analysis of recent works by leading scholars on destination governance was conducted. The synthesis of their thoughts provides valuable insights on the challenges of

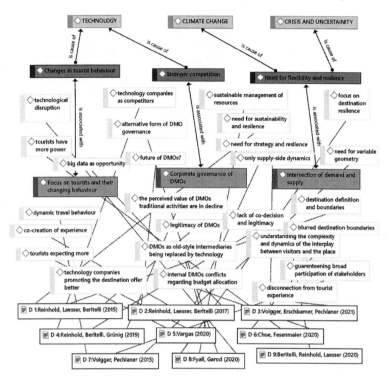

Figure 1.1 Content analysis of challenges in the works dealing with destination governance.

destination governance and their implications for further research (Figure 1.1).

Nowadays, we are witnessing the reinvention of tourist behaviour both in the theory and praxis (Cohen et al. 2014) formed by many factors, mainly by information technologies, shift in generational dominance and the rise of ethical concerns in consumption decisions. The development of information technologies in recent years, such as search engines, online travel agencies (OTAs), or social media has influenced the number of tourists around the world to use these technologies across the trip experience (Buhalis & Law 2008; Choe et al. 2017) and changed the tourist behaviour (Buhalis et al. 2011). Tourists seek more experience and want to be active in their creation (Xiang and Fesenmaier 2017b). Therefore, there is a need to co-create personalised experiences (Neuhofer et al. 2014) based on real-time big data analytics (Buhalis & Sinarta 2019). This dynamic change in tourist behaviour puts pressure on the network governance of destinations

(Volgger & Pechlaner 2015). Nowadays, it is more important than ever to better comprehend how tourists perceive and use ICTs to create and shape their trips (Femenia-Serra et al. 2018) in order to develop better destination governance based on their behaviour. Moreover, Cohen et al. (2014) emphasise that further research should focus on how technology impacts consumer behaviour as technological developments and the ways in which consumers deploy such developments continue to evolve. To progress in research, it is necessary to know in-depth the opinion and behaviour of tourists (Liberato et al. 2018) and their needs (Zhang et al. 2018), based on empirical research.

Further, more and more moderating actors in tourism networks, in particular DMOs, struggle with the tensions between guaranteeing broad participation of stakeholders, ensuring strategic alignment and providing space for innovations (Volgger & Pechlaner 2015). Traditional DMOs' activities (e.g. marketing, branding) are nowadays in decline due to the development of ICTs and more complex requirements of stakeholders and tourists (Reinhold et al. 2019). DMOs are seen as old-style intermediaries and tourists started to ignore them in favour of new technologies, where technology companies are seen as new competitors (Vargas 2020). DMOs struggle with internal conflicts regarding budget allocation, which require DMOs to prioritise each activity based upon strategic direction, cost and effectiveness of the effort. DMOs also lack the resources, control and legitimacy for functions assigned to them (Serra et al. 2017). All these factors create tensions in the corporate governance of DMOs (Reinhold et al. 2015), where DMOs are in search of a new model and role in a destination network, creating several implications for further research (Reinhold et al. 2018).

The third challenge of destination governance is the need for more focus on the intersection of tourism demand and supply. The concept of destination governance has focused mainly on the supply side of a tourism destination. However, as originally presented by Gunn (1972) and further developed by Beritelli and Laesser (2017), the foundation of destination development originates from demand-related challenges associated with tourist experiences. Therefore, the success of destinations depends on how suppliers respond to market dynamics and to changing tourist behaviour. In this regard, the process-oriented and flow-based view of tourism destinations, which conceptualise destinations as heterogeneous experience-scapes with multiple parallel supply networks, is recommended (Reinhold et al. 2020). On the one hand, the increased competition and blurred geographical boundaries of destinations require to focus more on cooperation

(Choe & Fesenmaier 2021). On the other hand, it is important to focus on visitor flows that activate the production process in a destination (Beritelli et al. 2019). In this sense, destination governance should steer visitors and set stages by understanding and intervening in a complex and dynamic ecosystem of exchange relationships in loosely identified destination boundaries by groups of suppliers connected by different visitor flows (Beritelli et al. 2020).

In the light of challenges that tourism destination governance has to face, the concept of destination design can help, integrating thinking on aesthetics, insights originating from recent advancements in technology and the established research tradition on destination development. This new perspective is based on inter- and trans-disciplinary thinking outside the known, providing flexible means for expressing and addressing complex issues in a human-centred and participatory manner (Volgger et al. 2021). As Volgger et al. (2021) further state, technology can help destination designers in familiarising themselves with the need of specific target groups and at the same time technology can be part of effective solutions. Therefore, the smart approach to destination governance with the help of design thinking can help to bring new ideas to destination development and help to cope with identified challenges.

References

Antonelli, G., and De Liso, N., 2016. Government and governance for smart development in smart communities. *In*: G. Antonelli, and G. Cappiello, eds. *Smart development in smart communities*. Oxfordshire: Routledge, 275–296.
Asero, V., Gozzo, S., and Tomaselli, V., 2016. Building tourism networks through tourist mobility. *Journal of Travel Research*, 55 (6), 751–763.
Axelrod, R., 1984. *The evolution of cooperation*. New York: Basic books.
Baggio, R., 2008. Symptoms of complexity in a tourism system. *Tourism Analysis*, 13 (1), 1–20.
Baggio, R., 2017. Network science and tourism – the state of the art. *Tourism Review*, 72 (1), 120–131.
Baggio, R., 2020. Tourism destinations: A universality conjecture based on network science. *Annals of Tourism Research*, 82 (April), 102929.
Baggio, R., and Del Chiappa, G., 2014. Real and virtual relationships in tourism digital ecosystems. *Information Technology and Tourism*, 14 (1), 3–19.
Baggio, R., and Scaglione, M., 2018. Strategic visitor flows and destination management organization. *Information Technology and Tourism*, 18 (1–4), 29–42.
Baggio, R., Scott, N., and Cooper, C., 2010. Network science. *Annals of Tourism Research*, 37 (3), 802–827.

Baggio, R., Scott, N., and Cooper, C., 2013. Using network analysis to improve tourist destination management. *In*: C. Costa, E. Panyik, and D. Buhalis, eds. *Trends in European tourism planning and organisation*. Bristol: Channel View Publications, 278–288.

Beritelli, P., 2011. Cooperation among prominent actors in a tourist destination. *Annals of Tourism Research*, 38 (2), 607–629.

Beritelli, P. and Bieger, T., 2014. From destination governance to destination leadership – Defining and exploring the significance with the help of a systemic perspective. *Tourism Review*, 69 (1), 25–46.

Beritelli, P., Bieger, T., and Laesser, C., 2007. Destination governance: Using corporate governance theories as a foundation for effective destination management. *Journal of Travel Research*, 46 (1), 96–107.

Beritelli, P., Crescini, G., Reinhold, S., and Schanderl, V., 2019. *How flow-based destination management blends theory and method for practical impact*. Cham: Springer, 289–310.

Beritelli, P., and Laesser, C., 2017. The dynamics of destinations and tourism development. *In*: D.R. Fesenmaier and Z. Xiang, eds. *Design science in tourism, tourism on the verge*. Cham: Springer International Publishing Switzerland, 195–214.

Beritelli, P., Reinhold, S., and Laesser, C., 2020. Visitor flows, trajectories and corridors: Planning and designing places from the traveler's point of view. *Annals of Tourism Research*, 82 (April), 102936.

Beritelli, P., Strobl, A., and Peters, M., 2013. Interlocking directorships against community closure: A trade-off for development in tourist destinations. *Tourism Review*, 68 (1), 21–34.

Bramwell, B., and Lane, B., 2011. Critical research on the governance of tourism and sustainability. *Journal of Sustainable Tourism*, 19 (4–5), 411–421

Buffa, F., Beritelli, P., and Martini, U., 2019. Project networks and the reputation network in a community destination: Proof of the missing link. *Journal of Destination Marketing and Management*, 11, 251–259.

Buhalis, D. and Law, R., 2008. Progress in information technology and tourism management: 20 years on and 10 years after the Internet – The state of eTourism research. *Tourism Management*, 29 (4), 609–623.

Buhalis, D., Leung, D., and Law, R., 2011. eTourism: Critical information and communication technologies for tourism destinations. *In*: Y. Wang and A. Pizam, eds. *Destination marketing and management: Theories and applications*. Wallingford: CAB International, 205–224.

Buhalis, D., and Sinarta, Y., 2019. Real-time co-creation and nowness service: Lessons from tourism and hospitality. *Journal of Travel & Tourism Marketing*, 36 (5), 563–582.

Burt, R.S., 1992. *Structural holes: The social structure of competition*. Cambridge: Harvard University Press.

Cehan, A., Eva, M., and Iațu, C., 2021. A multilayer network approach to tourism collaboration. *Journal of Hospitality and Tourism Management*, 46 (20), 316–326.

Choe, Y., and Fesenmaier, D.R., 2021. Designing an advanced system for destination management: A case study of Northern Indiana. *Industrial Management and Data Systems*, 121 (6), 1167–1190.

Choe, Y., Kim, J., and Fesenmaier, D.R., 2017. Use of social media across the trip experience: An application of latent transition analysis. *Journal of Travel and Tourism Marketing*, 34 (4), 431–443.

Coase, R., 1960. The problem of social cost. *Journal of Law and Economics*, 3 (1), 1–44.

Cohen, S.A., Prayag, G., and Moital, M., 2014. Consumer behaviour in tourism: Concepts, influences and opportunities. *Current Issues in Tourism*, 17 (10), 872–909.

Czernek-Marszałek, K., 2018. Cooperation evaluation with the use of network analysis. *Annals of Tourism Research*, 72, 126–139.

D'Agata, R., Gozzo, S., and Tomaselli, V., 2013. Network analysis approach to map tourism mobility. *Quality and Quantity*, 47 (6), 3167–3184.

d'Angella, F., and Go, F.M., 2009. Tale of two cities' collaborative tourism marketing: Towards a theory of destination stakeholder assessment. *Tourism Management*, 30 (3), 429–440.

Del Chiappa, G., and Baggio, R., 2015. Knowledge transfer in smart tourism destinations: Analyzing the effects of a network structure. *Journal of Destination Marketing and Management*, 4 (3), 143–144.

Del Chiappa, G., and Presenza, A., 2013. The use of network analysis to assess relationships among stakeholders within a tourism destination: An empirical investigation on Costa Smeralda-Gallura, Italy. *Tourism Analysis: An Interdisciplinary Journal*, 18 (1), 1–13.

Fayos-Solà, E., 2016. Governance. *In*: J. Jafari and H. Xiao, eds. *Encyclopedia of tourism*. Cham: Springer International Publishing, 399–401.

Femenia-Serra, F., García-Hernández, M., del Valle Tuero, E., and Perles-Ribes, J.F., 2018. Profiling tourists and their ICTs perception and use across Spanish destinations. *In*: *XII International Conference of Tourism and Information & Communication Technologies (Turitec)*. Malaga: Universtity of Malaga, Faculty of Tourism, 27–44.

Fyall, A. and Garrod, B., 2020. Destination management: A perspective article. *Tourism Review*, 75 (1), 165–169.

Fyall, A., Garrod, B., and Wang, Y., 2012. Destination collaboration: A critical review of theoretical approaches to a multi-dimensional phenomenon. *Journal of Destination Marketing and Management*, 1 (1–2), 10–26.

Gajdošík, T., 2015a. Socially responsible tourism destination governance. *In*: M. Gúčik, ed. *Folia turistica 6*. Belianum: Banská Bystrica, 25–31.

Gajdošík, T., 2015b. Network analysis of cooperation in tourism destinations. *Czech Journal of Tourism*, 4 (1), 26–44.

Gajdošík, T., Gajdošíková, Z., Maráková, V., and Borseková, K., 2017. Innovations and networking fostering tourist destination development in Slovakia. *Quaestiones Geographicae*, 36 (4), 103–116.

Gajdošík, T., Gajdošíková, Z., Maráková, V., and Flagestad, A., 2017. Destination structure revisited in view of the community and corporate model. *Tourism Management Perspectives*, 24 (October), 54–63.

Gibson, L., Lynch, P.A., and Morrison, A., 2005. The local destination tourism network: Development issues. *Tourism and Hospitality, Planning and Development*, 2 (2), 87–99.

Grama, C., and Baggio, R., 2014. A network analysis of Sibiu County, Romania. *Annals of Tourism Research*, 47, 89–93.

Gray, B., 1989. *Collaborating: Finding common ground for multiparty problems.* San Francisco: Jossey-Bass.

Gulati, R., 1998. Alliances and networks. *Strategic Management Journal*, 19 (4), 293–317.

Gunn, C., 1972. *Vacationscape: Designing tourist areas.* Austin: Bureau of Business Research, University of Texas at Austin.

Hall, C.M., 1999. Rethinking collaboration and partnership: A public policy perspective. *Journal of Sustainable Tourism*, 7 (3–4), 274–289.

Hall, C.M., 2008. *Tourism planning: Policies, processes and relationships.* 2nd edition Prentice Hall: Essex.

Hall, C.M., 2011. A typology of governance and its implications for tourism policy analysis. *Journal of Sustainable Tourism*, 19 (4–5), 437–457.

Hemmati, M., Dodds, F., Enayati, J., and McHarry, J., 2012. *Multi-stakeholder processes for governance and sustainability: Beyond deadlock and conflict.* Taylor & Francis Group.

Hoppe, B., and Reinelt, C., 2010. Social network analysis and the evaluation of leadership networks. *The Leadership Quarterly*, 21 (4), 600–619.

Hristov, D., and Zehrer, A., 2015. The destination paradigm continuum revisited: DMOs serving as leadership networks. *Tourism Review*, 70 (2), 116–131.

Jamal, T.B., and Getz, D., 1995. Collaboration theory and community tourism planning. *Annals of Tourism Research*, 22 (1), 186–204.

Kaspar, C., 1976. Le tourisme, objet d'étude scientifique. *The Tourist Review*, 31 (4), 2–5.

Keohane, R., and Nye, J.S., 1977. *Power and independence: World politics in transition.* Boston: Little, Brown and Company.

Kozak, M., Volgger, M., and Pechlaner, H., 2014. Destination leadership: Leadership for territorial development. *Tourism Review*, 69 (3), 169–172.

Kučerová, J., Gajdošík, T., and Schmidtová, I., 2018. Destination management and governance – Theory and practice in Slovakia. *In*: M. Boďa, ed. *Economic Theory and Practice 2017*. Banská Bystrica: Belianum, 305–316.

Laesser, C., Pfister, D., and Beritelli, P., 2019. Atmospheric turn and digitisation as chances for a sustainable destination management. *In*: Volgger, M., Pfister, D. (eds) *Advances in culture, tourism and hospitality research*. Emerald Publishing Limited, 177–193.

Leiper, N., 1979. The framework of tourism: Towards a definition of tourism, tourist, and the tourist industry. *Annals of Tourism Research*, 6 (4), 390–407.

Liberato, P., Alen, E., and Liberato, D., 2018. Smart tourism destination triggers consumer experience: The case of Porto. *European Journal of Management and Business Economics*, 27 (1), 6–25.

Magaš, D., and Meler, M., 2013. Creation of networks vs national tourism organization – Croatian experience. In: *2nd International Conference on Economics*. Dubai, 131–135.

Michálková, A., 2011. Strategic consideration of regional networks in tourism and their contradictory effects. *Ekonomicky Casopis*, 59 (3), 310–324.

Morrison, A.M., 2019. *Marketing and managing tourism destinations*. Oxon: Routledge.

Ness, H., Aarstad, J., Haugland, S., and Gronseth, B., 2014. Destination development. *Journal of Travel Research*, 53 (2), 183–195.

Neuhofer, B., Buhalis, D., and Ladkin, A., 2014. A typology of technology-enhanced tourism experiences. *International Journal of Tourism Research*, 16 (4), 340–350.

OECD, 2012. *OECD tourism trends and policies 2012*. Paris: OECD Publishing.

Palmer, A., 1996. Linking external and internal relationship building in networks of public and private sector organizations: A case study. *International Journal of Public Sector Management*, 9 (3), 51–60.

Palmer, A., 1998. Evaluating the governance style of marketing groups. *Annals of Tourism Research*, 25 (1), 185–201.

Pearce, D.G., 2014. Toward an integrative conceptual framework of destinations. *Journal of Travel Research*, 53 (2), 141–153.

Pearce, P., ed., 2019. *Tourist behaviour*. Cheltenham: Edward Elgar Publishing Limited.

Pechlaner, H., Beritelli, P., Pichler, S., Peters, M., and Scott, N., 2015. *Contemporary destination governance: A case study approach*. Emerald Group Publishing.

Pechlaner, H., Herntrei, M., Pichler, S., and Volgger, M., 2012. From destination management towards governance of regional innovation systems – The case of South Tyrol, Italy. *Tourism Review*, 67 (2), 22–33.

Pechlaner, H., and Innerhofer, E., 2018. Linking destinations and resilience – Challenges and perspectives. In: E. Innerhofer, M. Fontanari, and H. Pechlaner, eds. *Destination resilience*. London: Routledge, 3–13.

Pechlaner, H., Kozak, M., and Volgger, M., 2014. Destination leadership: A new paradigm for tourist destinations? *Tourism Review*, 69 (1), 1–9.

Pechlaner, H., Volgger, M., and Herntrei, M., 2012. Destination management organizations as interface between destination governance and corporate governance. *Anatolia*, 23 (2), 151–168.

Pfeffer, J., and Salancik, G., 1978. *The external control of organizations: A resource dependence perspective*. New York: Harper and Row.

Piere, J., and Peters, G., 2020. *Governance, politics and the state*. London: Red Globe Press.

Pike, S., 2008. *Destination marketing: An integrated marketing communication approach*. Burlington: Elsevier/Butterworth-Heinemann.

Pike, S., and Page, S.J., 2014. Destination marketing organizations and destination marketing: A narrative analysis of the literature. *Tourism Management*, 41, 202–227.

Plattner, M., 2013. Reflections on "governance". *Journal of Democracy*, 24 (4), 17–28.

Presenza, A., and Cipollina, M., 2010. Analysing tourism stakeholders networks. *Tourism Review*, 65 (4), 17–30.

Raisi, H., Baggio, R., Barratt-Pugh, L., and Willson, G., 2020. A network perspective of knowledge transfer in tourism. *Annals of Tourism Research*, 80 (March 2019), 102817.

Reinhold, S., Beritelli, P., and Grünig, R., 2019. A business model typology for destination management organizations. *Tourism Review*, 74 (6), 1135–1152.

Reinhold, S., Laesser, C., and Beritelli, P., 2015. 2014 St. Gallen consensus on destination management. *Journal of Destination Marketing & Management*, 4 (2), 137–142.

Reinhold, S., Laesser, C., and Beritelli, P., 2018. The 2016 St. Gallen consensus on advances in destination management. *Journal of Destination Marketing and Management*, 8, 426–431.

Reinhold, S., Laesser, C., and Beritelli, P., 2020. Flow-based destination management and marketing: A perspective article. *Tourism Review*, 75 (1), 174–178.

Rhodes, R.A.W., 2007. Understanding governance: Ten years on. *Organization Studies*, 28 (8), 1243–1264.

Ruhanen, L., Scott, N., Ritchie, B., and Tkaczynski, A., 2010. Governance: A review and synthesis of the literature. *Tourism Review*, 65 (4), 4–16.

Scott, N., Baggio, R., and Cooper, C., 2008. *Network analysis and tourism, from theory to practice*. Clevedon: Channel View Publications.

Scott, N., Cooper, C., and Baggio, R., 2008. Destination networks. Four Australian cases. *Annals of Tourism Research*, 35 (1), 169–188.

Scuttari, A., Pechlaner, H., and Erschbamer, G., 2021. Destination design: A heuristic case study approach to sustainability-oriented innovation. *Annals of Tourism Research*, 86 (June 2020), 103068.

Selin, S., and Beason, K., 1991. Interorganizational relations in tourism. *Annals of Tourism Research*, 18 (4), 639–652.

Serra, J., Font, X., and Ivanova, M., 2017. Creating shared value in destination management organisations: The case of Turisme de Barcelona. *Journal of Destination Marketing and Management*, 6 (4), 385–395.

Shaw, E., and Conway, S., 2000. Networking and the small firm. *In*: S. Carter and D. Jones-Evans, eds. *Entrerprise and small business*. Harlow: Prentice Hall.

Shields, B.P., Moore, S.A., and Eagles, P.F.J., 2016. Indicators for assessing good governance of protected areas: Insights from park managers in western Australia. *Parks*, 22 (1), 37–50.

Shih, H.Y., 2006. Network characteristics of drive tourism destinations: An application of network analysis in tourism. *Tourism Management*, 27 (5), 1029–1039.

Sørensen, F., and Balsby, N., 2020. Brokers and saboteurs: Actor roles in destination innovation network development. *Tourism Planning & Development*, 18 (5), 547–572.

Stoddart, M.C.J., Catano, G., Ramos, H., Vodden, K., Lowery, B., and Butters, L., 2020. Collaboration gaps and regional tourism networks in rural coastal communities. *Journal of Sustainable Tourism*, 28 (4), 625–645.

Tuohino, A., and Konu, H., 2014. Local stakeholders' views about destination management: Who are leading tourism development? *Tourism Review*, 69 (3), 202–215.

Tussyadiah, I.P., 2014. Toward a theoretical foundation for experience design in tourism. *Journal of Travel Research*, 53 (5), 543–564.

UNDP, 1997. *Reconceptualising governance*. New York: UNDP Bureau for policy and programme support.

Valeri, M., and Baggio, R., 2020a. Social network analysis: Organizational implications in tourism management. *International Journal of Organizational Analysis.*, 29 (2), 342–353.

Valeri, M., and Baggio, R., 2020b. Italian tourism intermediaries: a social network analysis exploration. *Current Issues in Tourism*, 0 (0), 1–14.

van der Zee, E., Gerrets, A.M., and Vanneste, D., 2017. Complexity in the governance of tourism networks: Balancing between external pressure and internal expectations. *Journal of Destination Marketing and Management*, 6 (4), 296–308.

Van der Zee, E., and Vanneste, D., 2015. Tourism networks unravelled; a review of the literature on networks in tourism management studies. *Tourism Management Perspectives*, 15, 46–56.

Vargas, A., 2020. Covid-19 crisis: A new model of tourism governance for a new time. *Worldwide Hospitality and Tourism Themes*, 12 (6), 691–699

Vernon, J., Essex, S., Pinder, D., and Curry, K., 2005. Collaborative policy-making: Local sustainable projects. *Annals of Tourism Research*, 32 (2), 325–345.

Volgger, M., Erschbamer, G., and Pechlaner, H., 2021. Destination design: New perspectives for tourism destination development. *Journal of Destination Marketing & Management*, 19(January), 100561.

Volgger, M., and Pechlaner, H., 2014. Requirements for destination management organizations in destination governance: Understanding DMO success. *Tourism Management*, 41, 64–75.

Volgger, M., and Pechlaner, H., 2015. Governing networks in tourism: What have we achieved, what is still to be done and learned? *Tourism Review*, 70 (4), 298–312.

Volgger, M., Pechlaner, H., and Pichler, S., 2017. The practice of destination governance: A comparative analysis of key dimensions and underlying concepts. *Journal of Tourism, Heritare and Services Marketing*, 3 (1), 18–24.

Williamson, O.E., 1975. *Markets and hierarchies: Analysis and antitrust implications*. New York: Free Press.

Wood, D.J., and Gray, B., 1991. Toward a comprehensive theory of collaboration. *Journal of Applied Behavioral Science*, 27 (2), 139–167.

Xiang, Z., and Fesenmaier, D., 2017a. Analytics in tourism design. *In*: Z. Xiang and D. Fesenmaier, eds. *Analytics in smart tourism design, tourism on the verge*. Cham: Springer International Publishing Switzerland, 1–10.

Xiang, Z., and Fesenmaier, D.R., 2017b. Big data analytics, tourism design and smart tourism. *In*: D.R. Xiang, Zheng, Fesenmaier, ed. *Annalytics in smart tourism design, concepts and methods*. Cham: Springer International Publishing Switzerland, 299–307.

Zehrer, A., and Raich, F., 2010. Applying a lifecycle perspective to explain tourism network development. *Service Industries Journal*, 30 (10), 1683–1705.

Zhang, T., Cheung, C., and Law, R., 2018. Functionality evaluation for destination marketing websites in smart tourism cities. *Journal of China Tourism Research*, 14 (3), 263–278.

2 Smart destination governance as a new model of destination development

The dynamic environment, in which DMOs now operate (Reinhold et al. 2019), pushes forward a new model of governance. Tourism literature stresses the crucial role of knowledge management and information and communication technologies in destination governance (Micera et al. 2013). ICTs are seen as a source of knowledge generation and dissemination that can help DMOs to reinforce their network value (Fuchs et al. 2014, Fortezza & Pencarelli 2018). Therefore, applying the developments arising from the application of smart tourism concept (Sheehan et al. 2016) is welcomed. This concept creates opportunities for better data collection and analysis. Although the smart concept has been considered in a few studies dealing with network science in tourism destinations (e.g. Baggio & Del Chiappa 2014; Raisi et al. 2018; Williams et al. 2017), the profound understanding of the potential of the smart initiative within this domain is still missing.

2.1 Smart tourism and its development

The smart concept has emerged as a result of the rise of information technology and the need for sustainability. It was originally derived from the UN Sustainable development goals and later it became a strategy that many times supersedes sustainability when describing development efforts (Joss et al. 2019). Smart development is generally discussed from two aspects. The first is connected with the development of information technologies that integrate hardware, software and network technologies to provide real-time awareness of the real world and advanced analytics to help people make more intelligent decisions about alternatives, as well as actions that will optimise business processes and business performances (Washburn et al. 2010). These technologies trigger innovation and lead to higher competitiveness while ensuring sustainable development (Aina 2017). Therefore,

DOI: 10.4324/9781003269342-4

the second aspect is related to the sustainability and the use of resources (Mehraliyev et al. 2019). Although sustainability is important, it is insufficiently addressed both in theory and practice (Gretzel 2021). As tourism is highly dependent on information technologies (e.g. Benckendorff, Sheldon, & Fesenmaier 2014; Buhalis 2003) and sustainable development of tourism is a prerequisite of its development (Hall 2019), the smart phenomenon has also penetrated into the tourism sector (Gajdošík 2018). Smart tourism is derived from the smart city agenda, paying special attention to tourists and their experience (Buhalis & Amaranggana 2014). As Gretzel (2021) states, while smart city development theory and practice have had 30 years to evolve, smart tourism as a concept has only existed for about 10 years. Thus, smart tourism lags behind smart city development. Academic interest in smart tourism can be documented using the basic search 'smart tourism' in documents indexed in the Scopus and Web of Science databases (Figure 2.1).

Smart tourism describes the current stage of tourism development influenced by the evolution of information technologies. It is a step in the evolution of information technologies in tourism in which the physical and governance dimensions of tourism are entering the digital playing field and new levels of intelligence are achieved (Gretzel 2011). It can be defined as integrated efforts to collect, aggregate, transform and distribute data using smart technologies with the goal of achieving efficiency, sustainability and enrichment of experience (Gretzel, Sigala, et al. 2015).

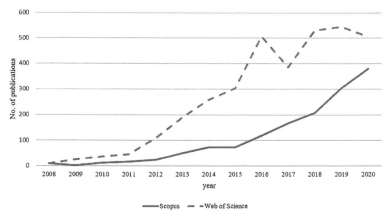

Figure 2.1 The evolution of academic interest in smart tourism.

Smart tourism is also related to the implementation of new technology-based governance and planning models (Lalicic & Önder 2018). In recent years, technologies have been so tightly knitted into the fabric of the travel experience and management of tourism products (Xiang et al. 2015) that they started to become central in the smart tourism concept (Ivars-Baidal et al. 2019). From a technological point of view, smart tourism can be seen as a direct extension of e-tourism.

E-tourism donates the analysis, design, implementation and application of information technologies/e-commerce solutions in the travel and tourism sector, as well as the analysis of the respective technical and economic processes and market structure (Werthner & Klein 1999). It comprises the digitisation of all processes and value chains in the tourism, travel, hospitality and catering industries. At the tactical level, it includes e-commerce and applies ICTs to maximise the efficiency and effectiveness of tourism organisations. At the strategic level, e-tourism revolutionises all business processes, the entire value chain, as well as the strategic relationships of tourism organisations with all their stakeholders (Buhalis 2003). E-tourism affects the costs, demand and competitiveness of tourism businesses (Zelenka 2012). Therefore, it can be stated that while e-tourism is more about digital connections, business processes and connecting stakeholders through the Internet, smart tourism is more about connecting physical objects with digital objects.

A smart tourism ecosystem is the most comprehensive way to describe the conceptual foundations of smart tourism. It is based on the idea that nothing works individually, but it interacts within the ecosystem to evolve. The ecosystem is composed of different types of species (customers, market players, government) that develop strong relationships in an inclusive environment based on specific activities and business networks (Moore 1993). Therefore, ecosystems could be a useful tool for better understanding the complex dynamics of smart tourism as they emphasise the holistic view.

The first attempt to apply the ecosystem concept to smart tourism was proposed by Zhang, Li, and Liu (2012), who proposed the basic concept of smart tourism based on the retrospect of the origin and development conditions of smart tourism and the comment of the available concept. Later, Zhu, Zhang, and Li (2014) expanded this concept by proposing five elements of smart tourism system: tourists, government, scenic zones, businesses and information exchange centres. Gretzel, Werthner, Koo, and Lamsfus (2015) developed a new model consisting of touristic consumers (tourists), residential consumers (residents), tourism suppliers (tourism businesses), suppliers from other industries, government, media, destination management organisations, digital technologies, all embedded in a space (tourism destination). Perfetto and Vargas-Sánchez (2018) proposed a three-level smart industrial heritage tourism business ecosystem. The most recent attempt (Gajdošík 2018) conceptualises the smart tourism ecosystem into four elements: (1) digital technologies used by (2) consumers (tourists, residents), (3) businesses (tourism businesses, businesses from other industries) and (4) tourism destination (space governed by DMO, government) (Figure 2.2).

Smart tourism is a phenomenon firmly grounded in *technology* (Gretzel, Reino, et al. 2015). Recent advances such as cloud computing, sensors and GPS widespread use, virtual and augmented reality and the full adoption of social media and mobile technologies have pushed the emergence of smartness in tourism (Xiang & Fesenmaier 2017). New digital technologies, or smart technologies, have introduced important innovations in various sectors and industries. The term 'smart technologies' does not indicate that the technology itself is smart, rather individuals and industry can become smarter when using it, as it enables to quickly correspond, sensitively analyse and predict occurring situations (Lee 2013). Smart technologies applied in the tourism sector are specific products and services that add value to tourist experiences in a concrete way by fostering higher interaction, co-creation and personalisation levels (Neuhofer et al. 2012). They offer significant opportunities for the management of businesses and destinations to enhance their competitiveness and offer a personalised experience for tourists to maximise their satisfaction (Gajdošík & Orelová 2020). Due to the ubiquitous role of technologies, the levels of experience have expanded since tourists have experience from the physical and virtual environments (Stare & Križaj 2018). Smart technologies are an ambiguous umbrella term for many advanced technologies that take connectivity to a further step (Femenia-Serra et al. 2018). Several terms can be used along with smart technologies (Table 2.1).

The *consumer level* is focused on providing intelligent support based on real-time and comprehensive understanding of the tourist experience (Xiang & Fesenmaier 2017) and by a better quality of life of residents. From the tourist point of view, information technologies should enhance the experience by providing all related real-time information about the destination and its services in the planning phase, enhance access to real-time information to assist tourists in exploring the destinations during the trip and prolong the engagement to relive the experience by providing descent feedback after the trip (Buhalis & Amaranggana 2015). The smart tourism concept anticipates that tourists are smart in the sense that they want to have a super-connected

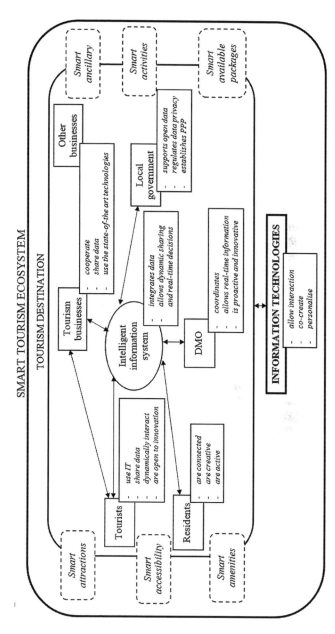

Figure 2.2 The concept of smart tourism ecosystem.

Table 2.1 Example of smart tourism technologies

Expression	Example of Technologies
Smart information and communication technologies Gretzel, Sigala, et al. (2015)	Sensors, big data, open data, Internet of Things, radio frequency identification, near-field communication, recommender systems, context-aware systems, autonomous agents, augmented reality, mobile and wearable devices, etc.
New technology trends in digital tourism Gelter (2017)	Wearables (watches, bracelets, glasses, lenses), augmented and virtual reality, 3D printing, artificial intelligence, e-agents, 3D holographic projection, accelerated mobile websites, cloud computing, big data analytics
Emerging technologies Ivars-Baidal et al. (2019)	QR codes, ambient intelligence, Fi-Ware, wearables, 3D printing, robots, open data, deep learning, real-time databases, Wi-Fi, mobile connection payments, BLE, augmented reality, Internet of Things, virtual reality, recommendations systems, cryptocurrencies, etc.
Smart tourism technologies Huang et al. (2017)	Destination apps, augmented and virtual reality, sensors, near-field communication, QR codes, iBeacons, ubiquitous connectivity through Wi-Fi, latest generation websites, social networks, chatbots, etc.
Technological advances and tools Sigala (2018)	Machine learning, artificial intelligence, industrial web, big data, Internet of Things, smart devices, robots, drones, beacons, virtual and augmented reality, near-field communications, ubiquitous computing, etc.
Smart tourism technologies Jeong and Shin (2020)	Ubiquitous computing, Internet of Things, cloud computing, ubiquitous connectivity through Wi-Fi, near-field communication, radio frequency identification, sensors, smartphones, mobile-connected devices, beacons, virtual reality, augmented reality, mobile apps, integrated payment methods, smart cards, social network sites, etc.
Disruptive technologies Buhalis (2020)	Internet of Things, Internet of Everything, 5G mobile network, radio frequency identification, mobile devices, wearable smartphones and devices, 3D printing, apps along with APIs, cryptocurrency and Blockchain, sensor and beacon networks, pervasive computing, gamification, analytical capabilities supported by artificial intelligence

experience (Femenia-Serra et al. 2018). 'Smart tourists' use information and communication technologies and look for a personalised tourism product in the form of experience (Gajdošík 2020). ICTs have been recognised as a major change of tourism experience (Prebensen & Foss 2011) and technology can function as an enabler, creator, attractor, enhancer, protector or even a destroyer of the experience (Benckendorff et al. 2014; Stipanuk 1993). Nowadays, tourists use different technologies for the experience. While latest generation websites with recommender systems and OTAs provide tourists with an easy access and booking of services, the use of augmented and virtual reality, mobile apps supported by ubiquitous connectivity through Wi-Fi or 4/5G network, destination smart cards and wearables enable to construct a new personalised experience. Moreover, tourists share their experiences live on social media (Wang et al. 2014) and by acquiring positive emotional support and encouragements from connected family and friends, these experiences are more enjoyable and memorable (Kim and Fesenmaier, 2017; Kim et al. 2013). Technologies have enabled tourists to become more involved and more innovative in creating their own experiences. Technologies have led to a significant shift in the roles of tourists from passive information recipients to active information co-creators (Choe et al. 2017; Wang et al. 2012). By using the mobile device and location-based services, tourists can exchange information in real time, be active in conversations and personalise the findings on the Internet. Moreover, technology enables to engage and explore more by providing useful context-based information (Neuhofer et al. 2014). Tourists, during their trip experience phases, contribute to the creation of data, which can be shared on a voluntary or non-voluntary basis. The willingness to share data with other stakeholders dynamically has been so far limited (Femenia-Serra et al. 2018), mainly due to privacy reasons. However, a growing trend has been observed among consumers in general, as they are becoming more open to sharing data (Pingitore et al. 2017). About 40% of consumers from Asia and Central and Eastern Europe (CEE) are willing to share data (Akselsen et al. 2015). This trend is expected to also evolve in tourism. The characteristics of a smart tourist can be summarised as follows (Table 2.2).

This connected, better informed and engaged tourist is dynamically interacting with the destination, leading to the need of co-creating tourism product and adding value for all tourism stakeholders (Neuhofer et al. 2012).

From the residents' point of view, information technologies should provide better services leading to an enhanced social and economic impact on the society (Abella et al. 2017). 'Smart residents' are constantly connected, creative and empowered enough, technology savvy and actively involved in the city (Hedlund 2012). However, Gretzel and Koo (2021) emphasise that smartification encourages tourism to spill into all areas of the city and blurs the boundaries between tourists and residents. Thanks to ICTs, residents have the ability to search for unusual tourist experiences, while tourists can find authentic experiences and 'live like a local'. This results in the convergence between 'everyday' and 'touristic', where, thanks to ICTs, residents are becoming

Table 2.2 Characteristics of a smart tourist

Description	Author(s)
An exigent and well-informed tourist, who is interested in the sustainability and responsibility of the destination he visits, yet he himself treats the environment with elevated sensibility and responsibility, as well. The smart tourist wants to interact with the destination. Due to this engagement, he himself becomes a co-creator and co-promoter of the destination.	Gahr et al. (2014)
A tourist heavily reliant on information and communication technologies, who undertakes in-depth information searches, and is very active on social media. Smart tourists are seeking customised and personalised offerings as well as mindful of value for money and safety and environmental matters.	Ghaderi et al. (2018)
A tourist who benefits from smart tourism by utilising various information technologies available at a smart tourist destination.	Gretzel et al. (2018)
A tourist who uses personalised and contextualised services, engage and explores the destination and is in search for authentic and immersive experience during all stages of travel.	Buhalis and Sinarta (2019)
A tourist being more knowledgeable of the destination, more demanding, better connected and more likely to share information, with a greater capacity for making recommendations and placing greater importance on user-generated content. Smart tourists differ from previous tourists, as they have become more dependent on information technology; self-service and reservation tools and they value easier access to technology, better value for their money, and greater variety, flexibility, personalisation and safety.	González-Reverté (2019)
A tourist who, by being open to sharing his or her data and making use of smart technologies, interacts dynamically with other stakeholders, co-creating in this way an enhanced and personalised smart experience. This tourist is open to innovations, social and pro-active and finds his or her natural environment in the smart tourism ecosystem and the smart destination.	Femenia-Serra et al. (2019)
A member of a profiling market segment, who is accustomed to use information technologies during all the trip experience phases. The willingness to co-create and share data leads to the need for personalised solutions, while reviews, authentic experiences and user-generated content are more crucial than in other segments in the destination selection process.	Gajdošík (2020)
A tourist that has at his/her service all digital tools provided by technologies to make every aspect of his/her life smarter and contribute to the wellbeing of the places visited. Smart tourists behave in a sustainable and responsible way.	Shen et al. (2020)

temporary tourists and tourists are becoming temporary residents. Therefore, it is dangerous to strictly separate tourists and residents in the smart context.

The *business level* is built on the access to shared data fostering cooperation and resource sharing among businesses (Xiang & Fesenmaier 2017). It incorporates the use of internal data and state-of-the-art technologies within businesses to support marketing, profitability and competitiveness, as well as data from an external environment supported by data sharing. 'Smart business' is capable of fully integrating internal and external applications and data exchange from the cloud, obtaining real-time and historical data from big data and applying interconnected and interoperable systems. This will support the interlink of value systems, improve the collective efficiency and profitability of the business ecosystem and strengthen the business competitiveness (Buhalis & Leung 2018). Studies focusing on open innovation and service-dominant logic could be useful for tourism businesses to identify, address and exploit the opportunities, challenges and affordances of smart tourism and to redefine their business models (Gretzel, Sigala, et al. 2015). However, research on smart tourism businesses is very scarce compared to other elements of the smart tourism ecosystem (Table 2.3).

Table 2.3 Characteristics of a smart business

Description	Author(s)
An establishment where a suite of smart technologies is used to inform operational decisions, ensure sustainability and enrich guest experience. It senses, reasons and acts. Moreover, it has a physical presence connected to a digital presence, both of which are interlinked with other actors as needed.	Gretzel (2016)
A knowledge-based, learning, open, networking organisation, following the rule of sustainable development in its operations and taking advantage of the achievements of technological progress.	Jeremen, Jędrasiak, and Rapacz (2016)
A new form of business combining modern information technology with tourism services, and taking tourists' experiences as a core element.	Li et al. (2017)
Moves from the logic of service to a logic focussed on experience. It focuses on offering a better experience through intelligent digitalisation.	Ballina (2020)

The *destination level* accompanies these previous two levels by increasing competitiveness and enhancing the quality of life of all stakeholders, including residents and tourists (Boes et al. 2016). The smart concept is applicable mainly for mature destinations, as they have the ability to focus on technology, knowledge and innovation that lead to smart development (Ivars-Baidal et al. 2019). Based on available data, the smart tourism initiative helps DMOs and destination stakeholders to make real-time decisions and adapt very fast to the changing environment. In a 'smart tourism destination', the DMO should function as a smart hub that coordinates all relevant information and makes it easily accessible for users to access them in real time. By digitalisation of core business processes, precise market targeting, service provision and proactiveness, it co-creates a tourism experience (Hedlund 2012). It should be the centre of excellence, as well as the innovation leader in tourism. The role of local government is to support open data, regulate data privacy and support public–private partnerships (Buhalis & Amaranggana, 2015; Hedlund, 2012). The holistic model that conceptualises smart tourism destination was proposed by Ivars-Baidal et al. (2019). This model is structured in three interrelated layers: (1) strategic-relational level – based on a governance characterised by public-private cooperation to obtain sustainable tourism development, (2) instrumental level – based on digital connectivity, sensorisation and big data which constitute the necessary infrastructure, (3) applied level – allows the development of solutions for increasing the efficiency of destination governance and enhancing tourist experience. Further, Gretzel et al. (2018) indicate that the role of smart destination is to lobby and partly sponsor the development of smart technology infrastructure and applications. This is done to curate and manage big data in a destination, in order to support the development and use of smart experiences by tourists and finally to link smart tourism with the overall quality of life and sustainability in a destination. Smart tourism destination creates a framework and plans for connecting business, technology and social infrastructures that make smartness possible (Shafiee et al. 2021). Smart destinations are considered a key piece of the smart tourism ecosystem and are principally based on the widespread use of technology and data by different stakeholders (Femenia-Serra et al. 2021) supporting the tourist experience and the local quality of life (Table 2.4).

Despite the fact that smartness is viewed mainly as focusing on new information technologies, it can be affirmed that technology is a necessary condition, but not sufficient to create smart tourism. It is also

Table 2.4 Characteristics of a smart destination

Description	Author(s)
A destination, where technology is being embedded in all organisations and entities, that is able to exploit synergies between ubiquitous sensing technology and their social components to support the enrichment of tourist experience.	Buhalis and Amaranggana (2014)
An innovative tourism destination built on an infrastructure of the state-of-the-art technology, which guarantees the sustainable development of tourism areas, facilitates the visitor's interaction with and integration into his or her surroundings, increases the quality of the experience at the destination and improves residents' quality of life.	Avila (2015)
An innovative tourist destination, built on an infrastructure of state-of-the-art technology guaranteeing the sustainable development of the tourist area, accessible to everyone, which facilitates the visitors' interaction with and integration into their surroundings, increases the quality of the experience at the destination, while also improving the quality of life of its residents	SEGITTUR (2015)
A tourism destination, combining the digital business ecosystem and network theories, where a networked system of stakeholders delivers services to tourists, complemented by a technological infrastructure aimed at creating a digital environment which supports cooperation, knowledge sharing and open innovation.	Del Chiappa and Baggio (2015)
A destination that facilitates tourist engagement and integration with the environment, enhances the quality of the tourist experience and improves the quality of life of the inhabitants of the destination.	Gretzel, Zhong, and Koo (2016)
A destination where knowledge and information are accessible to all stakeholders, facilitating them to carry out continuous innovation of their performance and activities, as much as possible.	Jovicic (2017)

important to stress the ability to share knowledge and innovation among destination stakeholders. Antonelli and Cappiello (2016) claim that smart development has three common elements: (1) centrality of technological innovation and growing potential of ICTs, (2) the role of networks that connect ICT with knowledge, (3) soft skills fostering innovation and knowledge transfer. Further, Boes et al. (2016) add that the use of information technologies is defined as 'hard smartness', while the soft aspect of smartness is also needed so that the right decisions can be made based on the data gained. This 'soft smartness' is fostered by open innovation, supported by investments in human and social capital and sustained by collaborative governance in order to develop the collective competitiveness to enhance social, economic and environmental prosperity for all stakeholders leading to sustainable competitive advantages.

Smart tourism should not be an ultimate goal, but with the help of technology, innovation and cooperation, it should bring a better tourist experience, the well-being of residents, enhance the effectiveness and competitiveness of businesses and destinations, and lead to sustainable, competitive and resilient development in a dynamic environment (Figure 2.3).

Moreover, to bring creative, practical and non-linear solutions (Brown 2008), as well as to better face the challenges, the smart concept should embrace design thinking. This symbiosis leads to the development of smart tourism design.

2.2 Foundations of smart tourism design

Huge and underlying changes in technological, socio-economic, environmental and political domains (Xiang et al. 2021) call for inter- and trans-disciplinary approaches that are able to deal with increased

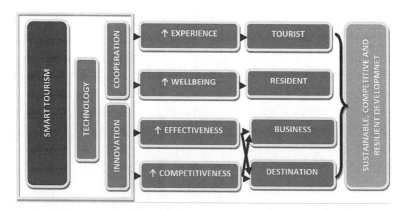

Figure 2.3 The goal of smart tourism.

complexity (Volgger et al. 2021) in the tourism system. To control and predict the behaviour of a system, approaches of design science are welcomed (Dresch et al. 2015). Design science is a relatively new, however, established discipline involving both creation and dissemination of knowledge. Design science is aimed at studying the creation of artefacts and their embedding in physical, psychological, economic, social and virtual environments. Moreover, a good design improves the systems through innovative and sustainable products and services, creates value and reduces the negative consequences of technology deployment. In design science, product and system design is addressed by combining analysis and synthesis, while drawing from many scientific disciplines (Papalambros 2015). The basic principles of design science are (1) experience orientation, (2) science-based, (3) employment of new tool and metrics (data analytics), (4) system orientation, (5) scalability and (6) orientation to action and change (Fesenmaier & Xiang 2017).

In the context of tourism, the design approach is derived from service design and experience design (Tussyadiah 2014). Service design is described as an outside-in perspective of service development in an organisation (Mager 2008). Service design takes into account customer journey and touchpoints (Zomerdijk & Voss 2010) while looking at services from the customer's point of view. Stickdorn, Schneider, Andrews, and Lawrence (2010) provide five foundational principles of service design: user-centricity, co-creation, sequencing, evidencing and holistic approach. Further, experience design started to be acknowledged with the rise of the experience economy (Pine & Gilmore 1999) and focus more on the quality of user experiences. Tourist experience is composed of micro-events that are sequenced as sensation, perception, emotion, cognition, memory and interpretation (Volo 2009), while the design framework embraces the mechanisms responsible for translating the objective (e.g. sensation) into subjective (emotion, fantasy and meaning). This translation is influenced by several factors. Fesenmaier and Xiang (2017) call it an experience production system, which consists of six components: (1) themes – guiding the perceptual process, (2) stories – building the connection between tourists and environment, (3) atmospherics – physical elements of a place, (4) affordances – understanding of an artefact, (5) co-creation – ability to interact with service providers and environment, (6) technology – facilitator of experience.

As understanding the nature of experience holds the key to effectively managing tourism destinations, tourist experience provides a vital foundation for the design of tourism places (Kim & Fesenmaier 2017). Therefore, design science in tourism is not only about supporting the tourist experience, but also provides a basic logic for conducting research and designing tourism places (Fesenmaier & Xiang 2017) based on design thinking. Design thinking uses sensibility and methods to match people's needs with what is technologically feasible and what a viable business strategy can convert into customer value and market opportunity. Design thinking also considers the human element and not only technology. Design thinking can be described as a system of spaces rather than a predefined series of orderly steps, while the spaces define different sorts of related activities that together form the innovation (Brown 2008). Design projects must pass through several spaces. Originally defined by Brown (2008) as inspiration, ideation and implementation, these spaces were further expanded by several authors (e.g. Serrat 2017) to define, research, ideate, prototype, choose, implement and learn.

The foundation of designing tourism places can be found in the work of Gunn (1972), who provided a new perspective for destination planning focusing on tourist experience. It was a significant change in thinking on how to address tourism planning, development and design by the inclusion of the idea of the tourism experience as a central theme in addressing opportunities being sought by tourists through the concept of 'vacationscape'. Further in his research, Gunn (1997) added that dealing with the variety of stakeholders in a destination tends to force thinking about innovation because traditional approaches do not work. This stresses the importance of gathering demand and supply data to assist in decision-making focused on development and design (O'Leary & Fesenmaier 2017). Building upon this knowledge, Scuttari, Pechlaner, and Erschbamer (2021) provide an approach to destination design, arguing that destination design is an active, creative, participatory and concurrent design of places, services and experiences focusing both on tourists and residents. It includes place design and collaborative design as a further development of spatial planning and community-based planning.

Design as a meta-discipline has the power to integrate sectoral thought and add creativity, non-linear approaches and transdisciplinary into the planning process, particularly when tackling sustainability issues (Scuttari et al. 2021). In this sense, design science can help smart tourism initiatives tackle the often overlooked sustainability concerns, therefore, creating the baseline for smart tourism design. The development of the Internet and smart technologies has made it possible to collect and analyse real-time, detailed tourist-related data. Thus, it creates opportunities to understand how tourists behave, thereby overcoming a number of limitations of previous methods of data collection and analysis in destination design (Xiang et al. 2021). This massive amount of data become fundamental for analytics in the field of tourism design (Lalicic et al. 2021). Therefore, the smart tourism approach provides opportunities for researchers and practitioners to collect and analyse tourism-related data almost anywhere and in real time, thus supporting the analytical approach to tourism design.

Smart tourism design is focused on the development of digital artefacts that support new and innovative processes, systems and experiences which can be used to reshape tourism (Xiang et al. 2021). It can be seen as a tool for a new understanding of problems and for creating new solutions based on an analytical approach. The smart tourism design system (Figure 2.4) is tourist-centric, technology- and data-oriented; embracing the experience, service, collaborative and place design.

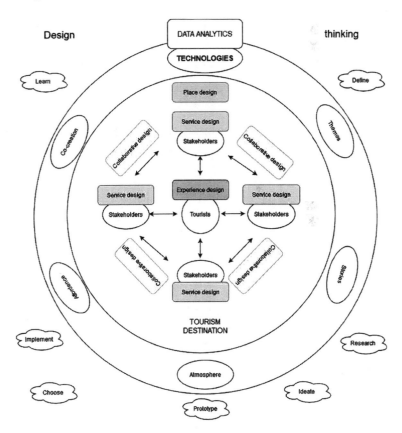

Figure 2.4 Smart tourism design system.

Smart tourism design embraces design thinking, focuses not only on how to enhance tourism experience, but also on how to effectively support the participation of stakeholders in collaborative and spatial planning (Scuttari et al. 2021) and with the help of state-of-the-art technologies and data analytics it develops a new measurement tool for destination development (Xiang et al. 2021).

2.3 The contribution of smart tourism design to destination governance

The smart tourism approach sets the requirements for tourism destinations to integrate physical, social and technological infrastructure in order to improve experiences for both tourists and residents and to adapt to the changing needs of destination stakeholders (Marsa-Maestre et al. 2008). Although technological resources are viewed as a necessary condition in the structure of the smart approach, in terms of destination success, there is social capital and governance that are also important factors (dos Santos Júnior et al. 2017). The pervasive role of ICTs with the combination of design thinking push forward a new model of governance – the smart governance.

Smart governance emerged with the rise of smart cities and is defined as a sociotechnical approach, which aligns technological potential with novel forms of collaboration between local government and citizens with the aim of tackling urban issues based on the principles of sustainability (Tomor et al. 2019). Smart governance can be viewed as the intelligent use of ICTs to improve decision-making (Pereira et al. 2018).

Starting from the smart city concept that addresses the urban challenges, smart destination governance includes structures and processes that are required for ensuring the commitment and effective coordination and integration of businesses, government and communities towards a holistic smart-oriented development plan for the tourism destination (Errichiello & Micera 2015). The governance of smart development is required to promote accessibility to information, transparency and public involvement in the decision-making process (Antonelli & Cappiello 2016). Gretzel and Scarpino (2018) highlight that smart governance is also transparent, accountable, collaborative and participatory. Smart tourism destination governance follows the new interpretation of a tourist as a co-creator; further, it builds on the need for greater integration among various stakeholders, the use of technological infrastructure creating digital environments that promote knowledge transfer and sharing, as well as the need to ensure sustainable and collaborative destination development (Errichiello & Micera 2021).

From a process-based perspective, smart destination governance focuses on sequential steps and tackles specific issues and variables to consider in the decision-making process of destination managers and other stakeholders required to build sustainable competitiveness of a destination. Based on a model of Wang and Xiang (2007) focusing on the collaboration process, Errichiello and Micera (2021) developed a smart tourism destination governance process framework consisting of assembling, ordering, implementation, evaluation and transformation steps. Moreover, taking into account the peculiarities of destination governance (Beritelli 2011) and building upon the recent studies focusing on measuring the progress of smart destinations (Femenia-Serra et al. 2021) and the smart design approach (Xiang et al. 2021) the process of smart tourism destination governance can be outlined (Figure 2.5)

Smart destination governance firmly places the DMO at the centre of smart tourism development (Gretzel 2022). The identified process of smart destination governance can lead to effective coordination of stakeholders in a destination stimulating the tourist experience, ensuring the well-being of residents and strengthening the competitiveness and sustainability of businesses and the destination. With the help of the smart design approach, the DMO and destination

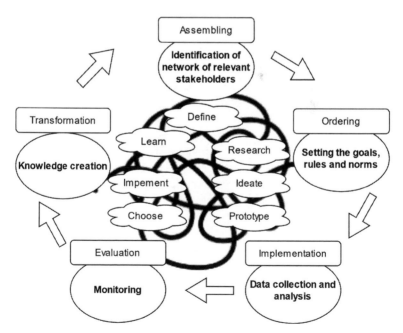

Figure 2.5 The process of smart tourism destination governance.

stakeholders have the capability to overcome the challenges that traditional destination governance has to face.

Smart destination governance puts forward the ability to gain and use the knowledge from available data with the support of ICTs (Shaw & Williams 2009) and use design thinking in order to create new solutions. The combination of smart infrastructure and interconnected systems effectively enables tourism destinations to optimise decisions based on gained knowledge, which in turn enhances tourist experience, offers business opportunities and improves destination governance in an intelligent way (Xiang et al. 2021). Based on the above mentioned, it can be summarised that smart destination governance includes processes and structures incorporating the network of all relevant stakeholders and focuses on non-linear decision-making based on available data in order to create knowledge and thus to overcome the challenges tourism destinations have to face.

The critical requirement of smart destination governance is to have sufficient knowledge about tourists and their behaviour (Choe & Fesenmaier 2021). In this sense, customer journey mapping can provide useful insights. It allows tourism practitioners and scholars to better comprehend customer steps towards achieving desirable experiences through several touchpoints, suggesting that touchpoints need to be intelligently integrated into the design process (Stare & Križaj 2018). Customer journey mapping in tourism generally involves researching and analysing the step-by-step process ranging from planning and booking to staying in a destination to sharing the experiences. It is a sequence of structured steps, grouped into different travel stages. To base the customer journey on solid research, observation, interviews or shadowing are used to gather the required information (Stickdorn & Schwarzenberger 2016). The customer journey framework is based on design principles, as they are customer-centric, precise, distinguish objective and subjective factors and provide visual representation (Halvorsrud et al. 2016). Destination managers can use tourist journey mapping based on market segments to identify different journeys, needs and touchpoints.

Secondly, the role of DMOs in a destination network is being questioned. In this sense, smart tourism design can provide new insights to data collection and analysis. Although network analysis is a widespread tool to analyse destination networks, the main problem with using the network approach in the context of tourism destination is data collection. Traditional methods of collecting data (e.g. surveys, archival records) provide past static data and their collection is many times time-consuming and misleading (e.g. high non-response rate in network surveys). The smart approach to network science can help to overcome this challenge. Moreover, after establishing the role of DMOs in the destination network, collaborative design can provide useful outcomes. The collaborative (or participatory) design adds creativity as a novel steering approach to install new networks and manage them in both linear and non-linear ways and shape governance systems, normally ruled by the steering mechanisms of trust, money, formal power and knowledge (Scuttari et al. 2021).

Lastly, the need for intersection of demand and supply in destination governance can be tackled by smart solutions. Demand perspective, represented by strategic visitor flows, can be empirically identified from information and data using selected informants that are in direct contact with tourists (e.g. receptionists, employees of tourist information centres, residents) (Beritelli et al. 2013). However, the use of big data and advanced analytics is welcomed. The supply-side perspective is represented by destination stakeholders. Using the service design principle allows using the service blueprinting approach in order to visualise processes based on the customer journey. The service blueprint is a tool to represent visually the meaningful moments of a service engagement from the customer perspective. The blueprint gives service providers a clear way to express their intentions and goals while linking them to the needs of customers (Meroni & Sangiorgi 2011). This flow-charting technique gives a clear insight into the processes of designing a tourist experience (Zehrer 2009). In terms of tourism destinations, service blueprinting emphasises the value of coordination and cooperation among the stakeholders that control the touchpoints along the tourist journey and allows stakeholders to recognise their roles in the co-creation of tourist experience (Beritelli et al. 2019).

It can be summarised that the contribution of smart tourism design to form smart destination governance lies in the human-centred, creative, interactive, visual and practical approach to finding the best ideas and solutions (Brown 2008). Design is more relational and innovative in comparison with traditional destination development methods. It is a way of expressing leadership through networks and linking spaces, artefacts and individuals (Volgger et al. 2021). Moreover, the smart approach to tourism destination governance has the ability to respond to the challenges that tourism destinations have to face. However, as Gelter et al. (2021) emphasise, the majority of existing research on smart tourism destinations is conceptual in nature. Therefore, there is a need to empirically analyse the contribution of the smart approach to overcome the identified challenges.

48   *The need for a new form of tourism*

References

Abella, A., Ortiz-de-Urbina-Criado, M., and De-Pablos-Heredero, C., 2017. A model for the analysis of data-driven innovation and value generation in smart cities' ecosystems. *Cities*, 64, 47–53.

Aina, Y.A., 2017. Achieving smart sustainable cities with GeoICT support: The Saudi evolving smart cities. *Cities*, 71 (August 2016), 49–58.

Akselsen, S., Martínez, H.C., Annunzio, A.D., Evjemo, B., and Menichelli, E., 2015. *Sharing for value.* Fornebu: Telenor Group.

Antonelli, G., and Cappiello, G., 2016. *Smart development in smart communities.* Oxfordshire: Taylor & Francis Group.

Avila, de L., 2015. *Smart destinations: XXI century toruism.* Lugano: Enter 2015.

Baggio, R., and Del Chiappa, G., 2014. Real and virtual relationships in tourism digital ecosystems. *Information Technology and Tourism*, 14 (1), 3–19.

Ballina, F.J., 2020. Smart business: The element of delay in the future of smart tourism. *Journal of Tourism Futures.* ahead of print.

Benckendorff, P., Sheldon, P., and Fesenmaier, D., 2014. *Tourism information technology.* Oxfordshire: CABI International.

Beritelli, P., 2011. Tourist destination governance through local elites - Looking beyond the stakeholder level Cumulative Postdoctoral Thesis Submitted by Center for Tourism and Transport From destination planning to destination management to destination governance Improving, (April).

Beritelli, P., Crescini, G., Reinhold, S., and Schanderl, V., 2019. *How flow-based destination management blends theory and method for practical impact.* Cham: Springer, 289–310.

Beritelli, P., Laesser, C., Reinhold, S., and Kappler, A., 2013. *Das St. Galler Modell fur Destinationsmanagement: Geschäftsmodellinnovation in Netzwerken.* St. Gallen: IMP-HSF.

Boes, K., Buhalis, D., and Inversini, A., 2016. Smart tourism destinations: Ecosystems for tourism destination competitiveness. *International Journal of Tourism Cities*, 2 (2), 108–124.

Brown, T., 2008. Design thinking. *Harvard Business Review*, 86 (6), 1–10.

Buhalis, D., 2003. *eTourism. Information technology for strategic tourism management.* Edinburgh: Pearson Education Limited.

Buhalis, D., 2020. Technology in tourism-from information communication technologies to eTourism and smart tourism towards ambient intelligence tourism: A perspective article. *Tourism Review*, 75 (1), 267–272.

Buhalis, D., and Amaranggana, A., 2014. Smart tourism destinations. *In:* Z. Xiang, and L. Tussyadiah, eds. *Information and communication technologies in tourism 2014.* Cham: Springer International Publishing, 553–564.

Buhalis, D., and Amaranggana, A., 2015. Smart tourism destinations enhancing tourism experience through personalisation of services. *In:* I. Tussyadiah, and A. Inversini, eds. *Information and Communication Technologies in Tourism 2015.* Cham: Springer International Publishing Switzerland, 377–389.

A new model of destination development   49

Buhalis, D., and Leung, R., 2018. Smart hospitality – Interconnectivity and interoperability towards an ecosystem. *International Journal of Hospitality Management*, 71 (April), 41–50.

Buhalis, D., and Sinarta, Y., 2019. Real-time co-creation and nowness service: Lessons from tourism and hospitality. *Journal of Travel & Tourism Marketing*, 36 (5), 563–582.

Choe, Y., and Fesenmaier, D.R., 2021. Designing an advanced system for destination management: A case study of Northern Indiana. *Industrial Management and Data Systems*, 121 (6), 1167–1190.

Choe, Y., Kim, J., and Fesenmaier, D.R., 2017. Use of social media across the trip experience: An application of latent transition analysis. *Journal of Travel and Tourism Marketing*, 34 (4), 431–443.

Del Chiappa, G., and Baggio, R., 2015. Knowledge transfer in smart tourism destinations: Analyzing the effects of a network structure. *Journal of Destination Marketing and Management*, 4 (3), 143–144.

dos Santos Júnior, A., Mendes Filho, L., Almeida García, F., and Simoes, J.M.M., 2017. Smart tourism destinations: A study based on the view of the stakeholders. *Revista Turismo em Análise -RTA*, 28 (3), 358–379.

Dresch, A., Lacerda, D.P., and Antunes, J.A.V., 2015. *Design science research: A method for science and technology advancement.* Cham: Springer International Publishing.

Errichiello, L. and Micera, R., 2015. Smart tourism destination governance. *In:* J. Spender, G. Schiuma, and V. Albino, eds. *FKAD 2015 International forum on knowledge asset dynamics. Culture, innovation and entrepreneurship: Connecting the knowledge dots.* Bari: IKAM – Institution of Knowledge Asset Management, 2179–2191.

Errichiello, L. and Micera, R., 2021. A process-based perspective of smart tourism destination governance. *European Journal of Tourism Research*, 29 (2021), 2909.

Femenia-Serra, F., Ivars-Baidal, J.A., Celdr, M.A., Perles-Ribes, F., and Giner, D., 2021. Measuring the progress of smart destinations: The use of indicators as a management tool. *Journal of Destination Marketing & Management*, 19 (2021), 100531.

Femenia-Serra, F., Neuhofer, B., and Ivars-Baidal, J.A., 2019. Towards a conceptualisation of smart tourists and their role within the smart destination scenario. *The Service Industries Journal*, 39 (2), 109–133.

Femenia-Serra, F., Perles-Ribes, J.F., and Ivars-Baidal, J.A., 2018. Smart destinations and tech-savvy millennial tourists: Hype versus reality. *Tourism Review*, 2 (June).

Fesenmaier, D.R., and Xiang, Z., 2017. Introduction to tourism design and design science in tourism. *In:* D. Fesenmaier, and Z. Xiang, eds. *Design science in tourism.* Cham: Springer, 3–16.

Fortezza, F., and Pencarelli, T., 2018. A comprehensive picture of the social media challenge for DMOs. *Anatolia*, 29 (3), 456–467.

Fuchs, M., Höpken, W., and Lexhagen, M., 2014. Big data analytics for knowledge generation in tourism destinations – A case from Sweden. *Journal of Destination Marketing & Management*, 3 (4), 198–209.

Gahr, D., Rodríguez, Y., and Hernández-Martín, R., 2014. Smart destinations. The optimisation of tourism destination management. *In: Seminario de economía canaria*. Tenerife, Islas Canarias, Spain.

Gajdošík, T., 2018. Smart tourism: Concepts and insights from Central Europe. *Czech Journal of Tourism*, 7 (1), 25–44.

Gajdošík, T., 2020. Smart tourists as a profiling market segment: Implications for DMOs. *Tourism Economics*, 26 (6), 1042–1062.

Gajdošík, T. and Orelová, A., 2020. Smart technologies for smart tourism development. *In*: R. Silhavy, ed. *Advances in intelligent systems and computing*. Cham: Springer, 333–343.

Gelter, H., 2017. *Digital tourism - An analysis of digital trends in tourism and customer digital mobile behaviour*. Oslo: Visit Artic Europe.

Gelter, J., Lexhagen, M., Fuchs, M., Gelter, J., Lexhagen, M., and Fuchs, M., 2021. A meta-narrative analysis of smart tourism destinations: Implications for tourism destination management implications for tourism destination management. *Current Issues in Tourism*, 24 (20), 2860–2874

Ghaderi, Z., Hatamifar, P., and Henderson, J.C., 2018. Destination selection by smart tourists: The case of Isfahan, Iran. *Asia Pacific Journal of Tourism Research*, 23 (4), 385–394.

González-Reverté, Francesc, 2019. Building sustainable smart destinations: An approach based on the development of Spanish smart tourism plans. *Sustainability*, 11 (23), 6874.

Gretzel, U., 2011. Intelligent systems in tourism: A social science perspective. *Annals of Tourism Research*, 38 (3), 757–779.

Gretzel, U., 2016. The new technologies tsunami in the hotel industry. *In*: M. Ivanova, S. Ivanov, and V.P. Magnini, eds. *The Routledge handbook of hotel chain management*. Oxon: Routledge, 516–523.

Gretzel, U., 2021. Smart tourism development. *In*: P. Dieke, B. King, and R. Sharpley, eds. *Tourism in development*. Oxford: CABI, 159–168.

Gretzel, U., 2022. The Smart DMO: A new step in the digital transformation of destination management organizations. *European Journal of Tourism Research*, 30 (2022), 3002–3002.

Gretzel, U., Ham, J., and Koo, C., 2018. Creating the city destination of the future: The case of smart Seoul. *In*: Y. Wang, A. Shakeela, A. Kwek, and C. Khoo-Lattimore, eds. *Managing Asian destinations. Perspectives on Asian Tourism*. Singapore: Springer, 199–214.

Gretzel, U. and Koo, C., 2021. Smart tourism cities: A duality of place where technology supports the convergence of touristic and residential experiences. *Asia Pacific Journal of Tourism Research*, 26 (4), 1–13.

Gretzel, U., Reino, S., Kopera, S., and Koo, C., 2015. Smart tourism challenges. *Journal of Tourism*, 16 (1), 41–47.

Gretzel, U., and Scarpino-Johns, M., 2018. Destination resilience and smart tourism destinations. *Tourism Review International*, 22 (3), 263–276.

Gretzel, U., Sigala, M., Xiang, Z., and Koo, C., 2015. Smart tourism: Foundations and developments. *Electronic Markets*, 25 (3), 179–188.

Gretzel, U., Werthner, H., Koo, C., and Lamsfus, C., 2015. Conceptual foundations for understanding smart tourism ecosystems. *Computers in Human Behavior*, 50, 558–563.

Gretzel, U., Zhong, L., and Koo, C., 2016. Application of smart tourism to cities. *International Journal of Tourism Cities*, 2 (2).

Gunn, C., 1972. *Vacationscape: Designing tourist areas.* Austin: Bureau of Business Research, University of Texas at Austin.

Gunn, C., 1997. *Vacationscape: Developing tourist areas.* 3rd edition. Washington: Routledge.

Hall, C.M., 2019. Constructing sustainable tourism development: The 2030 agenda and the managerial ecology of sustainable tourism. *Journal of Sustainable Tourism*, 27 (7), 1044–1060.

Halvorsrud, R., Kvale, K., and Følstad, A., 2016. Improving service quality through customer journey analysis. *Journal of Service Theory and Practice*, 26 (6), 840–867.

Hedlund, J., 2012. *Smart city 2020: Technology and society in the modern city.* Washington: Microsoft services.

Huang, C.D., Goo, J., Nam, K., and Yoo, C.W., 2017. Smart tourism technologies in travel planning: The role of exploration and exploitation. *Information and Management*, 54 (6), 757–770.

Ivars-Baidal, J.A., Celdrán-Bernabeu, M.A., Mazón, J.N., and Perles-Ivars, Á.F., 2019. Smart destinations and the evolution of ICTs: A new scenario for destination management? *Current Issues in Tourism*, 22 (13), 1581–1600.

Jeong, M., and Shin, H.H., 2020. Tourists' experiences with smart tourism technology at smart destinations and their behavior intentions. *Journal of Travel Research*, 59 (8), 1464–1477.

Jeremen, D.E., Jędrasiak, M., and Rapacz, A., 2016. The concept of smart hotels as an innovation on the hospitality industry market – Case study of puro hotel in Wrocław. *Economic Problems of Tourism*, 36 (4), 65–75.

Joss, S., Sengers, F., Schraven, D., Caprotti, F., and Dayot, Y., 2019. The smart city as global discourse: Storylines and critical junctures across 27 cities. *Journal of Urban Technology*, 26 (1), 3–34.

Jovicic, D.Z., 2017. From the traditional understanding of tourism destination to the smart tourism destination. *Current Issues in Tourism*, 3500, 1–7.

Kim, J., and Fesenmaier, D.R., 2017. Sharing tourism experiences. *Journal of Travel Research*, 56 (1), 28–40.

Kim, J., Fesenmaier, D.R., and Johnson, S.L., 2013. *The effect of feedback within social media in tourism experiences.* Berlin, Heidelberg: Springer, 212–220.

Lalicic, L., Marine-Roig, E., Ferrer-Rosell, B., and Martin-Fuentes, E., 2021. Destination image analytics for tourism design: An approach through Airbnb reviews. *Annals of Tourism Research*, 86 (November 2020), 103100.

Lalicic, L. and Önder, I., 2018. Residents' involvement in urban tourism planning: Opportunities from a smart city perspective. *Sustainability (Switzerland)*, 10 (6), 1852.

Lee, S.-H., 2013. Smart industries based on smart technologies in convergence. *Journal of Advanced Information Technology and Convergence*, 3 (1), 13–20.

Li, Y., Hu, C., Huang, C., and Duan, L., 2017. The concept of smart tourism in the context of tourism information services. *Tourism Management*, 58, 293–300.

Mager, B., 2008. Service design. *In*: M. Erlhoff and T. Marshall, eds. *Design dictionary*. Birkhäuser: Basel, 354–357.

Marsa-Maestre, I., Lopez-Carmona, M.A., Velasco, J.R., and Navarro, A., 2008. Mobile agents for service personalization in smart environments. *Journal of Networks*, 3 (5), 30–41.

Mehraliyev, F., Choi, Y., and Köseoglu, M.A., 2019. Progress on smart tourism research. *Journal of Hospitality and Tourism Technology*, 10 (4), 522–538.

Meroni, A. and Sangiorgi, D., 2011. *Design for services*. Surrey: Gower Publishing Limited.

Micera, R., Presenza, A., Splendiani, S., and Del Chiappa, G., 2013. SMART destinations: new strategies to manage tourism industry. *In*: G. Schiuma, J.C. Spender, and A. Pulic, eds. *IFKAD 2013: 8th International forum on knowledge asset dynamics. Smart growth: Organizations cities and communities.* Zagreb: IKAM - Institute of Knowledge Asset Management, 1405–1422.

Moore, J. F., 1993. Predators and prey: A new ecology of competition. *Harvard Business Review*, 71 (May-June), 75–86.

Neuhofer, B., Buhalis, D., and Ladkin, A., 2012. Conceptualising technology enhanced destination experiences. *Journal of Destination Marketing and Management*, 1 (1–2), 36–46.

Neuhofer, B., Buhalis, D., and Ladkin, A., 2014. A typology of technology-enhanced tourism experiences. *International Journal of Tourism Research*, 16 (4), 340–350.

O'Leary, J.T., and Fesenmaier, D., 2017. Concluding remarks: Tourism design and the future of tourism. *In*: D. Fesenmaier and Z. Xiang, eds. *Design science in tourism*. Cham: Springer, 265–272.

Papalambros, P., 2015. Design science: Why, what and how. *Design Science: An International Journal*, 1 (1), 1–38.

Pereira, G.V., Parycek, P., Falco, E., and Kleinhans, R., 2018. Smart governance in the context of smart cities: A literature review. *Information Polity*, 23 (2), 143–162.

Perfetto, M.C. and Vargas-Sánchez, A., 2018. Towards a smart tourism business ecosystem based on industrial heritage: Research perspectives from the mining region of Rio Tinto, Spain. *Journal of Heritage Tourism*, 13 (6), 1–22.

Pine, B.J., and Gilmore, J.H., 1999. *The experience economy: Work is theatre & every business a stage*. Brighton: Harvard Business School Press.

Pingitore, G., Rao, V., Cavallaro, K., and Dwivedi, K., 2017. *To share or not to share*. New York: Deloitte University Press.

Prebensen, N.K., and Foss, L., 2011. Coping and co-creating in tourist experiences. *International Journal of Tourism Research*, 13 (1), 54–67.

Raisi, H., Baggio, R., Barratt-Pugh, L., and Willson, G., 2018. Hyperlink network analysis of a tourism destination. *Journal of Travel Research*, 57 (5), 671–686.

Reinhold, S., Beritelli, P., and Grünig, R., 2019. A business model typology for destination management organizations. *Tourism Review*, 74 (6), 1135–1152.

Scuttari, A., Pechlaner, H., and Erschbamer, G., 2021. Destination design: A heuristic case study approach to sustainability-oriented innovation. *Annals of Tourism Research*, 86 (June 2020), 103068.

SEGITTUR, 2015. *Informe destinos turísticos inteligentes: construyendo el futuro*.

Serrat, O., 2017. Design thinking. *In*: Serrat, O., ed. *Knowledge solutions*. Springer Singapore: Singapore, 129–134.

Shafiee, S., Rajabzadeh Ghatari, A., Hasanzadeh, A., and Jahanyan, S., 2021. Smart tourism destinations: A systematic review. *Tourism Review*, 76 (3), 505–528.

Shaw, G. and Williams, A., 2009. Knowledge transfer and management in tourism organisations: An emerging research agenda. *Tourism Management*, 30 (3), 325–335.

Sheehan, L., Vargas-Sánchez, A., Presenza, A., and Abbate, T., 2016. The use of intelligence in tourism destination management: An emerging role for DMOs. *International Journal of Tourism Research*, 18 (6), 549–557.

Shen, S., Sotiriadis, M., and Zhou, Q., 2020. Could smart tourists be sustainable and responsible as well? The contribution of social networking sites to improving their sustainable and responsible behavior. *Sustainability (Switzerland)*, 12 (4), 1–21.

Sigala, M., 2018. New technologies in tourism: From multi-disciplinary to anti-disciplinary advances and trajectories. *Tourism Management Perspectives*, 25 (December 2017), 151–155.

Stare, M., and Križaj, D., 2018. Crossing the frontiers between touch points, innovation and experience design in tourism. *In*: A. Scupola, and L. Fuglsang, eds. *Services, experiences and innovation: Integrating and extending research*. Glos: Edward Elgar Publishing Ltd., 81–106.

Stickdorn, M., Schneider, J., Andrews, K., and Lawrence, A., 2010. *This is service design thinking: Basics, tools, cases*. Amsterdam: BIS Publishers.

Stickdorn, M., and Schwarzenberger, K., 2016. Service design in tourism. *In*: H. Siller and A. Zehrer, eds. *Entrepreneurship und tourismus: Unternehmerisches denken und erfolgskonzepte aus der praxis*. Wien: Linde Internationaô, 261–275.

Stipanuk, D.M., 1993. Tourism and technology: Interactions and implications. *Tourism Management*, 14 (4), 267–278.

Tomor, Z., Meijer, A., Michels, A., and Geertman, S., 2019. Smart governance for sustainable cities: Findings from a systematic literature review. *Journal of Urban Technology*, 26 (4), 3–27.

Tussyadiah, I.P., 2014. Toward a theoretical foundation for experience design in tourism. *Journal of Travel Research*, 53 (5), 543–564.

Volgger, M., Erschbamer, G., and Pechlaner, H., 2021. Destination design: New perspectives for tourism destination development. *Journal of Destination Marketing & Management*, (March), 100561.

Volo, S., 2009. Conceptualizing experience: A tourist based approach. *Journal of Hospitality and Leisure s*, 18 (2–3), 111–126.

Wang, D., Park, S., and Fesenmaier, D.R., 2012. The role of smartphones in mediating the touristic experience. *Journal of Travel Research*, 51 (4), 371–387.

Wang, D., Xiang. Z., and Fesenmaier, D.R., 2014. Adapting to the mobile world: A model of smartphone use. *Annals of Tourism Research*, 48, 11–26.

Wang, Y., and Xiang, Z., 2007. Toward a theoretical framework of collaborative destination marketing. *Journal of Travel Research*, 46 (1), 75–85.

Washburn, D., Sindhu, U., Balaouras, S., Dines, R.A., Hayes, N.M., and Nelson, L.E., 2010. *Helping CIOs understand "smart city" initiatives: Defining the smart city, its drivers, and the role of the CIO*. Cambridge, MA: Forrester research

Werthner, H., and Klein, S., 1999. *Information technology and tourism: A challenging relationship*. Wien: Springer.

Williams, N.L., Inversini, A., Ferdinand, N., and Buhalis, D., 2017. Destination eWOM: A macro and meso network approach? *Annals of Tourism Research*, 64, 87–101.

Xiang, Z., and Fesenmaier, D.R., 2017. Big data analytics, tourism design and smart tourism. *In*: D.R. Xiang, Zheng, Fesenmaier, eds. *Annalytics in smart tourism design, concepts and methods*. Cham: Springer International Publishing Switzerland, 299–307.

Xiang, Z., Stienmetz, J., and Fesenmaier, D.R., 2021. Smart tourism design: Launching the annals of tourism research curated collection on designing tourism places. *Annals of Tourism Research*, 86, 103154.

Xiang, Z., Tussyadiah, I., and Buhalis, D., 2015. Smart destinations: Foundations, analytics, and applications. *Journal of Destination Marketing and Management*, 4 (3), 143–144.

Zehrer, A., 2009. Service experience and service design: Concepts and application in tourism SMEs. *Managing Service Quality*, 19 (3), 332–349.

Zelenka, J., 2012. Informační a komunikační technologie – Perpetuum mobile cestovního ruchu. *Czech Journal of Tourism*, 1 (1), 5–17.

Zhang, L., Li, N., and Liu, M., 2012. On the basic concept of smarter tourism and its theoretical system. *Tourism Tribune*, 27 (5), 66–73.

Zhu, W., Zhang, L., and Li, N., 2014. Challenges, function changing of government and enterprises in Chinese smart tourism. *Enter* 2014.

Zomerdijk, L.G. and Voss, C.A., 2010. Service design for experience-centric services. *Journal of Service Research*, 13 (1), 67–82.

Part 2

The contribution of smart approach to overcoming the challenges of tourism destination governance

Digital transformation is altering governance models and tourism destinations need to grab the opportunities to better steer their development. The improved access to information through ICTs opens new opportunities to govern a destination. The smart approach is becoming a promising tool for overcoming the challenges that tourism destinations have to face. The smart approach is viewed as the ability of interconnected of technologies, to collect and analyse large amounts of variable data and to identify the insights to accomplish value maximisation for stakeholders (Buhalis 2020) with the help of design thinking. Moreover, a smart approach should ensure flexibility in decision-making and become able to translate these insights into novel collaborative ways of formulating and implementing policies (Herrschel 2018). Taking into account the design thinking, smartness should go beyond the data availability and focus also on shifting the competences to transcend inter-organisational relationships, while moving across borders and boundaries in a non-linear way (Herrschel 2018). In the context of tourism destination, it can be translated into data availability along the tourist journey, creation of new roles in destination networks, as well as the ability to cope with the dynamic construct of a destination.

The second part of the book empirically analyses the contribution of the smart approach to overcoming the identified challenges of tourism destination governance. It uses primary and secondary data sources from Slovakia. Slovakia was chosen as a reference country, where the use of Internet services and the integration of digital technology are at the average level of the European Union countries (European Commission 2019). The country is recognised as a digital challenger (Novak et al. 2018) and competitive in tourism in terms of the use of ICTs (Maráková 2021). This allows to analysing the real

DOI: 10.4324/9781003269342-5

conditions and problems of destination governance in various destinations, compared to analysis of best practices in smart tourism destinations (e.g. Seoul, Amsterdam, Benidorm). Moreover, the continuous formation of destination governance (Michálková et al.

2020) since the adoption of the market economy in the 1990s can provide useful information on the continuum between countries with developed tourism and developing countries (Gúčik 2020), thus serve as a living laboratory for destination governance analysis.

References

Buhalis, D., 2020. Technology in tourism-from information communication technologies to eTourism and smart tourism towards ambient intelligence tourism: A perspective article. *Tourism Review*, 75 (1), 267–272.

European Commission, 2019. *Digital economy and society index 2019. Country report Slovakia.*

Gúčik, M., 2020. *Tourism in the economy and society (Cestovný ruch v ekonomike a spoločnosti).* Bratislava: Wolters Kluwer.

Herrschel, T., 2018. Smart cities, towards smart governance? *In*: N. Dotti, ed. *Knowledge, policymaking and learning for European cities and regions: From research to practice.* Glos: Edward Elgar Publishing Ltd., 206–215.

Maráková, V., 2021. Competitiveness of Slovakia as a destination in the international tourism market. *In*: S.I. Bukowski, A. Hyz, and M.B. Lament, eds. *Competitiveness and economic development in Europe.* Oxon: Routledge, 247–257.

Michálková, A., Kubičková, V., and Gáll, J., 2020. Sectoral tourism concentration in the context of the regional policy. *Ekonomicky Casopis*, 68 (10), 1105–1125.

Novak, J., Purta, M., Marciniak, T., Ignatowicz, K., Rozenbaum, K., and Yarwood, K., 2018. *The rise of digital challengers. How digitization can become the next growth engine for Central and Eastern Europe.* Atlanta: McKinsey & Company.

3 Changing tourist behaviour along the tourist journey

Tourists are nowadays more active and have higher expectations in terms of tourism experience. The widespread adoption and use of information technologies have resulted in a radical shift in tourist behaviour. Technologies help tourists to participate in the creation of a personalised experience during the journey. Understanding their experience can be done by analysing the customer journey concept, embracing all the interactions between the tourist and destination stakeholders. Throughout a tourist journey, the tourist is in contact with both direct (or tangible) cues (e.g. products) and indirect (or intangible) cues (e.g. feelings and emotions). These direct and indirect cues are encountered across the tourist journey and act as touchpoints shaping the trip-experience phases (planning, booking and staying) (Stocchi et al. 2016). The concept of touchpoints puts the tourist at the focus of the analysis. As smart destination governance is user-centric and based on data analytics, it is important to analyse the possibilities of data collection within the touchpoints along the tourist journey and to find out the behaviour of different market segments.

The empirical analysis is based on the two-step questionnaire survey. The first step was done in 2018 by obtaining information from 5,975 tourists. The overall quota sampling was used to obtain a reasonably sound approximation of the population concerning the age and education of respondents, as these two variables are crucial in technology usage and acceptance (Czaja et al. 2006; Ellis & Allaire 1999). One year later, technology savvy market segments were contacted with a more in-depth survey focusing on the impact of information technologies on the travel and specific ways of co-creation. Such an empirical analysis is important, as it enables to find out the demand perspective on smartness, valuable for decision-making of DMOs and destination stakeholders.

DOI: 10.4324/9781003269342-6

3.1   Touchpoints and possibilities of data collection along the tourist journey

At each stage of the tourist journey, from the planning phase, through booking, on-site services use, till post-trip experience sharing, tourists are in contact with several organisations. Moments of contact are represented by different touchpoints. These touchpoints can also be treated as communication channels (Halvorsrud et al. 2016). They are points of contact or media where a customer comes into touch with a stakeholder or its employees, products or brand. This point can trigger positive or negative experiences that can strengthen or weaken the customer relationship (Neslin et al. 2006). Along the touchpoints, several data of personal, behavioural or geographic character can be collected to support the smart tourism initiative (Gajdošík 2019). In this way, it is important to find out the significance of these touchpoints from a tourist point of view and to analyse the possibilities of data collection.

The analysed 5,975 tourists were asked to provide the significance of touchpoints for creating the experience based on their previous journey on the scale of 1–5 (1 – unimportant, 5 – the most important). Further, the answers were analysed using descriptive statistics and touchpoints were graphically represented based on the phases of the tourist journey (Figure 3.1).

During the planning and booking phase, the most significant are search engines (e.g. Google), friends and relatives (word of mouth), hotel websites, Internet distribution systems (IDS, e.g. booking.com) and online travel agencies (OTA, e.g. Expedia). Moreover, tourists are also searching for information on social networks (e.g. Facebook), in travel agencies, on destination web and review sites (e.g. TripAdvisor). In recent years, the significance of sharing economy platforms (e.g. Airbnb) and meta search engines (e.g. Trivago) has been increasing steadily. The analysis confirmed that the role of information technologies in the pre-trip phase is gaining momentum, as the Internet offers a rich atmosphere for prospective tourists to gain familiarity, harvest and retrieve travel-related information and resources (Elci et al. 2017).

During the stay in a destination, tourists consider the direct contact with stakeholders and their employees as the most important touchpoint. This direct contact occurs during the use of facilities (e.g. accommodation, catering) and engagement with the service in order to fulfil the primary tourism needs. This behaviour is similar to shopping behaviour, where people value the physical stores as the most

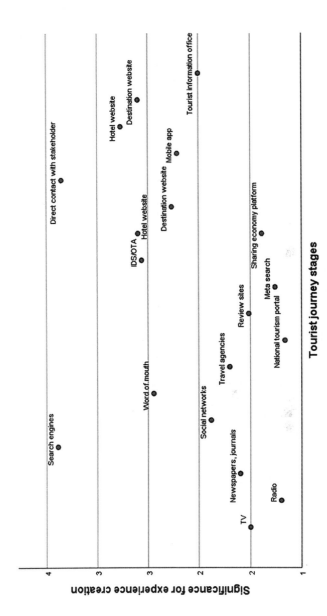

Figure 3.1 Significance of different types of touchpoints during the tourist journey.

important touchpoints along their journey in town centres (Stocchi et al. 2016). In order not to get lost in an unfamiliar environment of a destination, tourists use mainly hotel and destination websites, which provide important information on services and enable co-creation of experience, while the mobile apps integrate all the above-mentioned services. Tourists also contact physically tourist information offices to find information and assistance. This behaviour reflects the fact that ICTs in some way function as a tourist information office, albeit without human touch. The online channels are becoming more like virtual destinations, where tourists can also experience the places online (Morrison 2019), get relevant information and co-create their experience.

The analysis revealed ICTs play an important role as touchpoints in a destination. The digital environment provides tourists a plethora of ways to interact with the destination and its stakeholders. Moreover, the use of ICTs has shifted tourist expectations and changed their behaviour. Tourists can instantly find information, compare products and prices in different destinations and also within a destination. They can read customer testimonials, post reviews and share conversations with friends in real time. Therefore, the rise of ICTs changes the situation in a destination. Due to ICTs, the destination and its stakeholders have the power to provide a personalised experience based on data aggregation. This experience is data-driven, context-aware and co-created with tourists in real time (Neuhofer et al. 2015) (Figure 3.2).

With the help of research on the significance of different types of touchpoints along the tourist journey, the most important sources of data can be identified. The sources of data include web and social media, sensors, mobile devices, wearables and cards. These sources produce valuable data, which are inevitable for smart destination governance.

The *web and social media* play an important role mainly in searching and booking phases. Search engines and IDS/OTA provide valuable data on tourist search behaviour and booking. The data can include the most used keywords and information on tourist booking trends (e.g. booking ID, booked services in destinations). Moreover, social media provide valuable information. Instead of tourist demographic and psychographic characteristics (age, gender, preferences), social media provide a large amount of unstructured data from reviews and comments. These data can also include text reviews or geotagged material (photos, videos, check-ins). Despite the high

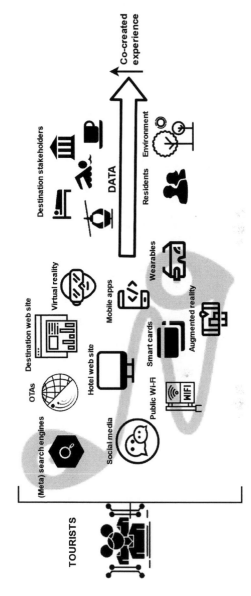

Figure 3.2 Using ICTs along tourist journey.

applicability of geotagged information in the smart approach, it has several limitations: (1) the data sparsity issues (i.e. extremely few records for individuals), (2) potential bias of the sample who posted on social media during the trip compared to population, (3) few online sources to access geotagged photos (Wong et al. 2017). Nevertheless, social media is a particularly prevalent touchpoint in the tourist journey and their ability to provide different types of data makes them a valuable information source capable of strengthening the smart destination governance.

Destination and hotel websites are generators of more specific data. These can include IP address, bounce rate, page time view, reservation ID and many others. These information can be accessed by simple analytical tools (e.g. Google Analytics). Along with these websites, external websites can also be valuable sources of data. As tourism is heavily dependent on the weather, data collection from weather portals is also important. Moreover, information about destination competitors published on the web is also valuable for governing a destination.

In order to acquire such information, web scraping and web crawling are used. Web scraping technology recognises different types of data on the website and saves only specified data, while web crawling identifies other pages which should be scraped and thus build a large collection of data from the web. The web crawler (or robot and spider) program can be implemented to iteratively and automatically download websites, extract URLs (Uniform Resource Locators) from their hypertext mark-up language (HTML) and fetch them (Li et al. 2018). Data from social media can be extracted using application programming interfaces (APIs). Several social media (e.g. Twitter, Flickr) provide easily data collection through APIs; however, others (e.g. Instagram) have some restrictions.

In addition to the web and social media, useful sources of data on tourist behaviour are *sensors* embedded throughout the destination environment. Sensors installed in tourism destinations include sensors to monitor traffic, energy, air quality or sensors for density of crowds (Table 3.1).

These sensors can monitor tourist behaviour during the stay in a destination, as well as the whole environment of the destination using cameras, scanners, infrared ports, radio frequency identifications (RFID), near-field communication (NFC), Wi-Fi hotspots, Bluetooth low energy (BLE) beacons, satellite technologies and other sensing technologies. People are tracked using cameras and scanners, while

Table 3.1 Example of sensors embedded throughout destination environment in selected tourism destinations

Destination	Example Sensors
Barcelona	• sensors to monitor traffic • smart streetlight sensors • air quality monitoring sensors
Amsterdam	• sensors for density of crowds • identification and traceability sensors based on BLE (beacons)
Helsinki	• sensors for energy monitoring
Singapore	• sensors and cameras for cleanliness • sensors for density of crowds • sensors to monitor traffic
Salzburg	• traffic sensors • energy monitoring sensors

mobile devices are tracked by sensing technologies (e.g. GPS, Bluetooth), or by GSM network. The sensing technologies are enabled by destination apps and allow real-time location or mobility traces, as well as context-aware surveys. The data can be collected along with user ID and timestamp and saved into the app, which can be accessed by the app developer. Although there are several geolocation-based techniques that can track tourists, the most appropriate one is the tracking of mobile phone users (Padrón-Ávila & Hernández-Martín 2020).

Tracking mobile devices using GSM networks is known as mobile positioning. Positioning data can be tracked actively, using a tracking system, or passively, when data are stored in mobile network operators' databases. For destinations, the passive way is more acceptable, as the data are stored each time a person uses actively the mobile phone (call, messaging, using the mobile Internet). This method can become an interesting and pertinent tool for monitoring spatial behaviour and can enlarge traditional and volunteered geographical information (through social media and mobile apps) data sources. Among the advantages, there is data collection for larger territory, spatial and temporal precision is higher than for regular tourism statistics (Baggio & Scaglione 2018). The indicators include the number of unique tourists, the number of visits to a given destination, the exact number of nights spent at a destination or travel trajectories. Data can be classified by country of origin, according to time (day, week, month) or space (GPS coordinates), duration of the stay (same-day visitors, overnight stays), destination (primary destination, secondary destination, transit), etc. However, due to privacy, processing has to guarantee anonymity when the visitor cannot be directly or indirectly identified.

Tracking wearable devices is another way of collecting data on tourists. While smartwatches offer similar data as mobile devices, smart glasses can provide video files of tourist attractions that are really spotted by tourists. Tracking the cards is also useful for obtaining data on tourist behaviour. Destinations can use the tracking of bank cards or destination smart cards. If tracking a bank card, data are stored in a bank each time a customer uses the point-of-sale (POS) terminal or ATM extraction with a payment card. The biggest advantage is that POS and ATMs are geo-localised. Consumption can also be classified according to the country of residence of the visitor, the holiday place, consumed services or other visitor characteristics. Destination smart card validators are used to read these cards and to collect logs from transactions. Apart from basic analytics such as the number of issued cards and the number of guests (broken down to new/recurrent, or by accommodation and country), other approaches can be used to analyse the behaviour of tourists. However, similar privacy regulations have to be used as in dealing with mobile positioning data. The overall list of data concerning different sources is presented in Figure 3.3.

ICTs provide data on tourist behaviour, movement and visitation of tourist attractions valuable for destination stakeholders. Technology represents an opportunity to actively participate in destination activities and to take part in the design of its own experience (Prebensen et al. 2013). Tourists are becoming co-designers, co-marketers, co-advertisers, co-promoters and co-distributors of tourism experience (Sigala 2018). They show proactiveness in terms of content and communication with stakeholders. They are becoming active managers, not only consumers but also producers and developers of tourism activity. Based on the data collected along their journey, personalisation strategies for better governance can be launched, including tracking (data collection) profiling (data analysis) and matching (individualisation). However, in order to launch personalisation strategies, DMOs and destination stakeholders should know at first the behaviour of different tourist segments concerning the technology use and find out if these segments are suitable to focus on.

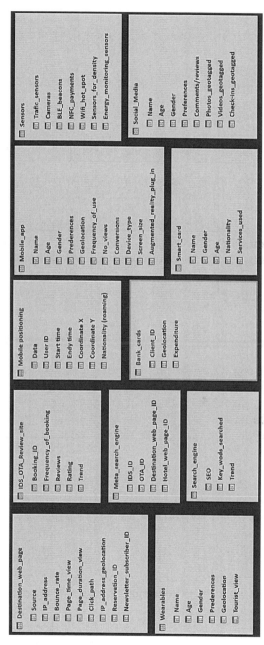

Figure 3.3 Sources of data collection and data characteristics.

3.2 Behaviour of different tourist segments along the tourist journey

The analysis of touchpoints and possibilities of data collection revealed the most important sources of data inevitable for smart destination governance. However, the analysis gives only general information on tourist behaviour and the possibility of its analysis. To better tailor services and be more competitive, destinations should have information about their main market segments. In light of the dynamic environment, destination managers should segment tourists based on their experiences, rather than socio-demographic characteristics (Choe et al. 2017).

In order to segment the analysed tourists, three characteristics were used – the use of technologies, co-creating and willingness of data sharing. These characteristics mirror the tourist behaviour in the smart tourism ecosystem. A two-step cluster analysis was performed. The number of clusters was chosen according to Schwarz's Bayesian Criterion (BIC), which indicated a six-segment solution. The silhouette measure of cohesion and separation of the two-step cluster analysis reached the value of 0.70, indicating good cluster quality. Subsequently, the analysed tourists were divided into six segments. For better characteristics, the mean values and standard deviations of psychographic characteristics concerning technology acceptance, co-creating and sharing were calculated (Table 3.2).

These characteristics were used to describe different clusters and with the help of the theory of technology acceptance (Venkatesh et al. 2003, Benckendorff et al. 2005), the six segments were created. As these segments are accessible, measurable and substantial, as well as distinct and suitable in size, they can be treated as tourist market segments. This kind of segmentation helps to focus on homogenous groups, find their specific behaviour and make it possible to better tailor services.

In order to graphically display the differences among the segments in technology use, co-creation and sharing, the 3D scatter plot was used (Figure 3.4).

Tourists can be classified into the following segments:

- *No-sharers* (segment 1) are tourists who appreciate the use of technologies, use them also during their stay in the destination for co-creation; however, they have a fear of data sharing and prefer privacy.

Table 3.2 Profile of the sample and the clusters regarding the technology use, co-creating and sharing

Cluster		Total	1	2	3	4	5	6	Kruskal–Wallis	
		N = 5,975 (100%)	N = 1,075 (17.99%)	N = 800 (13.39%)	N = 862 (14.43%)	N = 1,178 (19.72%)	N = 1,222 (20.45%)	N = 840 (14.06%)	χ^2	p-value
Technology use and acceptance	x̄	2.22	2.49	3.00	0.81	2.00	2.47	2.57	3926.46	0.000
	s	0.31	0.50	0.00	0.39	0.00	0.49	0.49		
Co-creating	x̄	1.29	3.06	0.32	0.79	0.36	0.38	3.13	4002.73	0.000
	s	0.61	1.42	0.16	0.37	0.17	0.16	1.4		
Sharing	x̄	1.02	0.72	0.74	0.58	0.54	1.70	1.83	2287.28	0.000
	s	0.45	0.38	0.45	0.25	0.22	0.68	0.74		

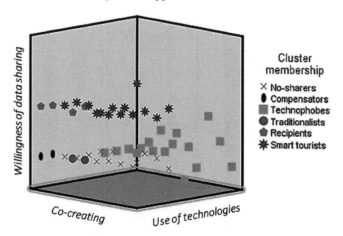

Figure 3.4 The visualisation of clusters.

- *Compensators* (segment 2) are interested in technologies, use them in everyday life, but try to avoid them during travel, seeking for 'digital detox'.
- *Technophobes* (segment 3) do not use or accept technologies in their lives and during travel.
- *Traditionalists* (segment 4) are good at technology use but do not want to share data and co-create the products during the holidays. Travelling is a time to relax for them.
- *Recipients* (segment 5) are very good at technology use and want to share their basic as well as more personal information. They look for standardised products, as they are passive information recipients.
- *Smart tourists* (segment 6) are very good at information technologies, looking for personalised products resulting from co-creation. They share their basic and more personal data, some of them also the real-time position.

In order to examine deeply the behaviour of different segments, the further analysis is focused on their characteristic travel behaviour (Table 3.3) in comparison with other segments. Kruskal–Wallis and Chi-square tests were used to show the existence of statistically significant differences between the segments.

In the pre-trip phase, all market segments use information technologies for searching information, planning the trip and booking services. While planning and booking, the hotel website is the most

Table 3.3 Profile of the sample and the clusters regarding socio-demographic characteristics and the use of technologies during trip experiences phases

Cluster	Total sample	1	2	3	4	5	6	Kruskal–Wallis	
	N = 5,975 (100%)	N = 1,075 (17.99%)	N = 800 (13.39%)	N = 862 (14.43%)	N = 1,178 (19.72%)	N = 1,222 (20.45%)	N = 840 (14.06%)		
	%	%	%	%	%	%	%	χ²	p-value
Socio-demographic characteristics									
Age	42.35	41.94	36.59	50.17	44.07	40.36	40.89	494.49	0.000
Salary	1136.52	1155.63	1218.38	964.09	1120.42	1176.64	1173.87	166.20	0.000
Consumption	136.09	142.92	135.42	122.24	131.66	135.32	149.56	67.16	0.000
Planning and booking									
IDS/OTA	1.56	1.67	1.73	0.95	1.28	1.76	2.02	364.404	0.000
Hotel web site	1.59	1.88	1.48	1.33	1.44	1.52	1.94	231.936	0.000
Destination web site	1.26	1.61	1.06	1.12	1.15	1.04	1.65	287.524	0.000
Meta search	0.61	0.88	0.47	0.5	0.49	0.5	0.85	174.710	0.000
Sharing economy platform	0.39	0.64	0.47	0.17	0.16	0.35	0.57	248.745	0.000
Staying in a destination									
Digital map	1.24	1.54	1.38	0.74	1.02	1.23	1.56	691.966	0.000
Hotel web site	0.86	1.19	0.68	0.56	0.68	0.78	1.27	621.879	0.000
Destination app	0.53	1.20	0.17	0.32	0.18	0.20	1.22	2217.018	0.000
Destination web site	0.77	1.13	0.56	0.49	0.6	0.62	1.21	739.188	0.000
Smart cards	0.41	0.93	0.10	0.26	0.14	0.14	0.99	1864.164	0.000
Wearables	0.19	0.50	0.03	0.10	0.02	0.03	0.50	1096.523	0.000
Sharing the experiences									
Social media	1.02	0.73	0.74	0.58	0.54	1.70	1.83	2287.275	0.000

important touchpoint for smart tourists, no-sharers and recipients. IDS/OTA is used quite often by smart tourists, recipients, compensators and no-sharers. Destination websites attract mainly smart tourists and compensators. Other touchpoints, such as meta-search and sharing economy platforms, are used only sometimes by all identified segments. These findings are in line with the research of Amaro and Duarte (2015), who state that favourable attitude and compatibility with the lifestyle of Internet users are the key factors that influence to purchase travel online, as smart tourists, no-sharers and recipients have a positive attitude to ICTs and their lifestyle includes online presence.

In order not to get lost in an unfamiliar environment, the used information technologies help tourists to solve problems in real time, provide flexibility and experience enrichment. During the stay at a destination, the main source of information is a digital map. This finding supports the research of Park (2014) who claims that digital maps belong to the most useful travel features. Smart tourists and no-sharers also use quite often the hotel website and the destination app. Destination apps enable to concentrate all the important tourist information about a destination in one place and can support the co-creation and personalisation of the experience. Moreover, maps play a major role in spatially edging tourist experiences (Farías 2011), thus contributing to the overall tourist experience. Smart cards are also useful for these market segments. Smart cards can reveal important information about tourist behaviour in a destination (e.g. movement, product and services used) and promote the most important tourism offer. Tourists can focus more on experiencing rather than searching for tourist attractions and finding the appropriate transport mode. Moreover, the destination website is important for technology savvy segments – smart tourists, no-sharers and recipients. This creates opportunities for changing destination websites into smart portals providing convenience to technology aware tourists by filtering suitable information and learning from the processes to provide users with explicit and customised information. As a result of technology shrinking, wearables started to be used by technology savvy tourists. These devices are predicted to have a significant impact on the interaction with the surroundings of a destination (Tussyadiah 2014) in the near future.

The use of social media to share the experience is very often by smart tourists and recipients. These segments trust the reviews and recommendations of other tourists published on social media. Writing and publishing post-trip experiences can help tourists to strengthen and build experience, and at the same time have an impact on decision-making of other tourists (Shen et al. 2020). The overall results of all market segments in sharing the experience after the trip are in line with the findings of Choe et al. (2017), who state that one-third of tourists use at least one type of social media for their trip-related behaviours after the trip.

When choosing a destination (Table 3.4), the most important decisive factors among all market segments are reviews, price and authentic experience. For smart tourists, reviews are more important than price, while for other market segments, the price factor outperforms the other factors. Thanks to information technologies, reviews are up-to-date and visible to all tourists. Moreover, as Xiang and Gretzel (2010) state, tourists consider reviews to be a more reliable source of information than other sources. Reviews and recommendations for future intentions to travel to a destination from social media have an impact on prospective tourists (Volo 2010), mainly smart tourists.

The offer of authentic experience is important for almost the majority of market segments except for technophobes. This segment takes more into account the recommendation from family and friends. The majority of tourists are keen on memorable activities and experiences that influence the senses and create a relationship with the destination. This finding supports the shift towards the experience economy (Pine & Gilmore 1999), where the offering is staging or producing experience. It is in line with the research of Kumar et al. (2014), who demonstrate that people derive more happiness from the anticipation of experiential purchases and that waiting for an experience tends to be more pleasurable and exciting than waiting to receive a material good. Moreover, interactivity, personalisation and informativeness gained by the use of ICTs are the key factors that affect tourist experience (Jeong & Shin 2020).

Official photos and videos of a destination are slowly being replaced by customer photos and videos. Marketer-generated media content is being challenged by user-generated content (UGC), as the real-time aspect and objectivity are more appealing to tourists. Ease of reservation is equally important for almost 30% of tourists, while other factors, such as travel distance, customer service and sustainable principles, do not play such an important role when choosing a destination, as less than 20% of tourists consider them as an important decisive factor.

The analysis of technology use among specified segments revealed that technology plays an important role in the travel journey of smart

Table 3.4 Profile of the sample and the clusters regarding the factors influencing the choice of a destination

Cluster	Total	1	2	3	4	5	6	Chi-square test	
	N = 5975 (100%)	N = 1075 (17.99%)	N = 800 (13.39%)	N = 862 (14.43%)	N = 1178 (19.72%)	N = 1222 (20.45%)	N = 840 (14.06%)		
	%	%	%	%	%	%	%	χ^2	p-value
Reviews	0.81	0.78	0.83	0.66	0.76	0.84	0.88	242.984	0.000
Price	0.88	0.88	0.9	0.86	0.87	0.9	0.86	16.259	0.006
Authentic experience	0.50	0.49	0.54	0.38	0.49	0.54	0.55	70.937	0.000
Recommendations from family and friends	0.37	0.37	0.35	0.39	0.35	0.37	0.41	9.754	0.083
Official photos and videos	0.33	0.31	0.34	0.26	0.30	0.38	0.37	46.152	0.000
Customer photos and videos	0.29	0.29	0.31	0.18	0.21	0.38	0.37	166.76	0.000
Ease of reservation process	0.31	0.33	0.30	0.29	0.30	0.31	0.34	9.308	0.097
Travel distance	0.17	0.16	0.15	0.25	0.17	0.16	0.16	45.039	0.000
Customer service	0.05	0.06	0.05	0.05	0.04	0.05	0.09	28.397	0.000
Sustainable principles	0.04	0.05	0.03	0.03	0.03	0.04	0.06	19.244	0.002

tourists, no-sharers and recipients. These market segments account for 52.50% of the market. They have the highest spending on additional services in a destination, making them economically interesting segments. These tourists are not confused in an unfamiliar environment and want to have a personalised experience. The most important decisive factors of destination selection are reviews, price and authentic experience. Moreover, the findings stress that the smart tourism initiative is not only pushed from the supply side, but also from the demand side. These findings are important for advancing smart destination governance. In this regard, further analysis is focused on the behaviour of technology savvy tourists.

3.3 Technology savvy tourists and their behaviour

The consequent survey was made among technology savvy tourists (smart tourists, no-sharers and recipients). Members of these segments were contacted with a more in-depth survey in 2019. Finally, 499 responses were obtained. Firstly, these tourists were asked to give their opinion regarding the expected degree of impact of selected technologies on tourism development and anticipate the period of maximum impact in tourism (Figure 3.5).

Social media, public Wi-Fi, latest generation websites as well as mobile apps are considered technologies with the highest impact in a short time. These technologies are already implemented in many destinations; however, they should be enriched by location-based services, real-time conversation and artificial intelligence-based applications. Therefore, if a destination wants to attract technology savvy tourists, it should invest more in its official tourism website and better manage its online reputation.

Technologies enhancing tourist experience (smart cards, recommender systems, online assistance, chatbots, virtual assistance, wearables and augmented and virtual reality) have been predicted to have a slightly lower impact and destinations should implement them soon (in 2–3 years) to satisfy the demand of technology savvy tourists.

Technologies related to data management and storage, such as destination management system, e-reputation management, cloud computing, blockchain and open data are also considered as technologies with medium expected impact within 2 or 3 years. These technologies are prerequisites of big data analytics that can analyse and interpret data on tourist behaviour in a destination. Therefore, if a destination wants to offer a personalised tourism product, it is inevitable to start using these technologies.

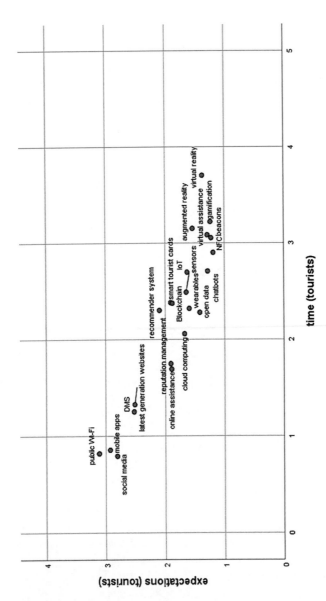

Figure 3.5 Evaluation of technologies by technology savvy tourists.

Note: Expectation – expected degree of impact measured on a scale: 0 – no impact, 4 – very high impact. Time – anticipated period of maximum impact measured on a scale: 0 – today, 2 – short term/2–5 years/, 5 – medium term /5–10 years, 10 – long term/10 years and more.

Technology savvy tourists consider the sensing and network technologies (NFC, beacons, sensors) as being more important in the time range of 3–4 years. The effect of these technologies can be enhanced using the Internet of Things, which allows collected data to be transferred to data management systems. This analysis revealed the specific technologies with their period of implementation. This can be helpful for DMOs and destination stakeholders.

The use of ICTs by technology savvy tourists serves as a prerequisite for experience co-creation. These tourists do not want to be passive information recipients; however, a shift towards active co-creation and personalisation of experience is seen. From the technological point of view, there are several requirements for experience co-creation. Firstly, it is the information aggregation based on data from tourists (Neuhofer et al. 2015). There are several ways, how tourists share their data in order to co-create. Nowadays, the most important is enabling cookies on websites and location-based services in mobile apps or creating an account on a website. These tourists are quite active in conversations with tourism producers through social media and some tourists enable mobile apps to provide personal information from smartphone databases (Figure 3.6).

Instead of obtaining data from tourists themselves, a destination can also obtain relevant information about their behaviour from other sources. As mentioned previously, these sources include sensors, mobile positioning or cards. Tourism destinations can use sensors for monitoring traffic or density of crowds. These sensors can monitor tourist behaviour using cameras, scanners, infrared ports, radio frequency identification, near-field communication, Wi-Fi hotspots, beacons and other sensing technologies. Moreover, mobile positioning can be used to track tourist mobile devices. In order to monitor tourist purchase behaviour, tracking the bank or tourist cards is also useful.

However, data sharing is influenced by the fear of misusing the data. On the one hand, 29.7% of technology savvy tourists do not have such a fear. On the other hand, 43.4% of these tourists are afraid of overall privacy evasion and 24.3% do not want their movement to be monitored. This creates some challenges for co-creation that destinations have to face.

The co-creation of experience also requires that stakeholders are dynamically connected in a system to facilitate personalised experiences (Buhalis & Amaranggana 2015) and real-time synchronisation (Neuhofer et al. 2015). The real-time databases for monitoring and big data analytics should be implemented in destinations to create the baseline for such a synchronisation, thus enabling the real-time

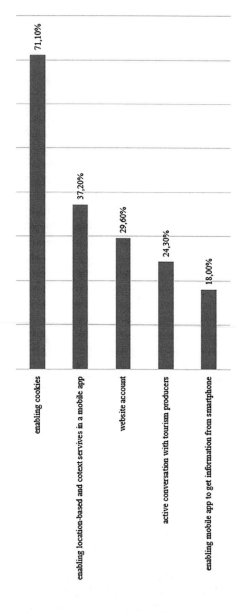

Figure 3.6 Using information technologies for experience co-creation by technology savvy tourists.

experience co-creation. The co-creation adds value to tourists as it ensures the experience is unique, authentic and memorable. It also leads to higher satisfaction and provides better economic value for a destination and its stakeholders. However, smartness should not be viewed only from the lens of information technology. Respecting the principles of sustainability is also important. Tourists should not use technologies merely for their own enjoyment, they should also behave sustainably during all trip experience phases. The analysis revealed that the technology savvy market segments are more likely to choose a destination that behaves sustainably than other segments. Information technologies have put into the hands of these tourists more powerful tools providing more efficient and effective alternatives in all trip experience phases. This creates additional possibilities for sustainable behaviour (Table 3.5).

The used technologies (e.g. search engines, websites, social media, IDS/OTA) during planning and booking enable tourists to easily find and compare destinations based on sustainable principles. When staying at the destination, tourists are more informed thanks to sensors, destination apps and smart cards. Such an informed tourist can make better decisions by reducing traffic congestion or overcrowding of tourist attractions in peak periods. Thanks to sharing economy platforms (e.g. Airbnb, VizEat, TourByLocals), tourists have direct contact with local culture, thus supporting the residents and avoiding the crowding-out effect. Sharing the experience is also an important part

Table 3.5 The impact of technologies on sustainable behaviour of tourists

Trip Experience Phase	Sustainable Behaviour	Example of Technology
Planning and booking	- easier finding and comparing destinations and their products based on respecting sustainable principles	- search engines, websites, social media, IDS/ OTA
Staying in a destination	- making better decisions based on information (reducing traffic congestion, or overcrowding) - enabling contact with local culture and supporting the local economy	- sensors, destination apps, smart cards, sharing economy platforms
Sharing the experience	- influencing other tourists to behave in a sustainable way by active real-time conversation	- social media

of sustainable tourist behaviour. Regular use of social media for sharing the sustainable experience is influencing other tourists to behave more sustainably.

In summary, the analysis of the behaviour of different market segments revealed that the smart tourism initiative is also pushed by the demand side, as the majority of tourists use ICTs along their journey. The use of information technologies during all the trip experience phases provides valuable data and strengthens the effectiveness and governance of a destination. The technology savvy segments are active co-creators of their experience and behave in a more sustainable way.

These findings support the need for smart destination governance and the need for destination design based on tourist experience.

References

Amaro, S., and Duarte, P., 2015. An integrative model of consumers' intentions to purchase travel online. *Tourism Management*, 46 (1), 64–79.

Baggio, R., and Scaglione, M., 2018. Strategic visitor flows and destination management organization. *Information Technology and Tourism*, 18 (1–4), 29–42.

Benckendorff, P., Moscardo, G., and Murphy, L., 2005. High tech versus high touch: Visitor responses to the use of technology in tourist attractions. *Tourism Recreation Research*, 30 (3), 37–47.

Buhalis, D., and Amaranggana, A., 2015. Smart tourism destinations enhancing tourism experience through personalisation of services. *In*: Tussyadiah, L., Inversini, A., eds. *Information and communication technologies in tourism 2015*. Cham: Springer International Publishing, 377–389.

Choe, Y., Kim, J., and Fesenmaier, D.R., 2017. Use of social media across the trip experience: An application of latent transition analysis. *Journal of Travel and Tourism Marketing*, 34 (4), 431–443.

Czaja, S.J., Charness, N., Fisk, A.D., Hertzog, C., Nair, S.N., Rogers, W.A., and Sharit, J., 2006. Factors predicting the use of technology: Findings from the Center for Research and Education on Aging and Technology Enhancement (CREATE). *Psychology and Aging*, 21 (2), 333–352.

Elci, A., Abubakar, A.M., Ilkan, M., Kolawole, E.K., and Lasisi, T.T., 2017. The impact of travel 2.0 on travelers booking and reservation behaviors. *Business Perspectives and Research*, 5 (2), 124–136.

Ellis, R.D., and Allaire, J.C., 1999. Modeling computer interest in older adults: The role of age, education, computer knowledge, and computer anxiety. *Human Factors: The Journal of the Human Factors and Ergonomics Society*, 41 (3), 345–355.

Farías, I., 2011. Tourist maps as diagrams of destination space. *Space and Culture*, 14 (4), 398–414.

Gajdošík, T., 2019. Big data analytics in smart tourism destinations. A new tool for destination management organizations? *In*: V. Katsoni, and M. Segarra-Oña, eds. *Smart tourism as a driver for culture and sustainability*. Springer, Cham, 15–33.

Halvorsrud, R., Kvale, K., and Følstad, A., 2016. Improving service quality through customer journey analysis. *Journal of Service Theory and Practice*, 26 (6), 840–867.

Jeong, M., and Shin, H.H., 2020. Tourists' experiences with smart tourism technology at smart destinations and their behavior intentions. *Journal of Travel Research*, 59 (8), 1464–1477.

Kumar, A., Killingsworth, M.A., and Gilovich, T., 2014. Waiting for Merlot: Anticipatory consumption of experiential and material purchases. *Psychological Science*, 25 (10), 1924–1931.

Li, J., Xu, L., Tang, L., Wang, S., and Li, L., 2018. Big data in tourism research: A literature review. *Tourism Management*, 68, 301–323.

Morrison, A.M., 2019. *Marketing and managing tourism destinations*. Oxon: Routledge.

Neslin, S.A., Grewal, D., Leghorn, R., Shankar, V., Teerling, M.L., Thomas, J.S., and Verhoef, P.C., 2006. Challenges and opportunities in multichannel customer management. *Journal of Service Research*, 9 (2), 95–112.

Neuhofer, B., Buhalis, D., and Ladkin, A., 2015. Smart technologies for personalized experiences: A case study in the hospitality domain. *Electronic Markets*, 25 (3), 243–254.

Padrón-Ávila, H., and Hernández-Martín, R., 2020. How can researchers track tourists? A bibliometric content analysis of tourist tracking techniques. *European Journal of Tourism Research*, 26 (2020), 1–30.

Park, J., 2014. Hotel mobile apps: Most requested features Available at: https://www.innovimobile.com/hotelmobile-apps-requested-features (accessed 20 November 2018).

Pine, B.J., and Gilmore, J.H., 1999. *The experience economy: Work is theatre & every business a stage*. Brighton: Harvard Business School Press.

Prebensen, N.K., Vittersø, J., and Dahl, T.I., 2013. Value co-creation significance of tourist resources. *Annals of Tourism Research*, 42, 240–261.

Shen, S., Sotiriadis, M., and Zhang, Y., 2020. The influence of smart technologies on customer journey in tourist attractions within the smart tourism management framework. *Sustainability (Switzerland)*, 12 (10), 1–18.

Sigala, M., 2018. New technologies in tourism: From multi-disciplinary to anti-disciplinary advances and trajectories. *Tourism Management Perspectives*, 25, 151–155.

Stocchi, L., Hart, C., and Haji, I., 2016. Understanding the town centre customer experience (TCCE). *Journal of Marketing Management*, 32 (17–18), 1562–1587.

Tussyadiah, I., 2014. Expectation of travel experiences with wearable computing devices. *In*: Z. Xiang, and I. Tussyadiah, eds. *Information and communication technologies in tourism 2014*. Cham: Springer International Publishing Switzerland, 539–552.

Venkatesh, V., Morris, M., Davis, G., and Davis, F., 2003. User acceptance of information technology: Toward a unified view. *MIS QUARTERLY*, 27 (3), 425–478.

Volo, S., 2010. Bloggers' reported tourist experiences: Their utility as a tourism data source and their effect on prospective tourists. *Journal of Vacation Marketing*, 16 (4), 297–311.

Wong, E., Law, R., and Li, G., 2017. Reviewing geotagging research in tourism. *In*: R. Shegg, and B. Stangl, eds. *Information and communication technologies in tourism 2017*. Cham: Springer International Publishing, 43–58.

Xiang, Z., and Gretzel, U., 2010. Role of social media in online travel information search. *Tourism Management*, 31 (2), 179–188.

4 The impact of smart tourism ecosystem on the role of destination management organisation

The smart tourism ecosystem challenges the role of DMOs in tourism destinations. Destinations, as an important element of the smart tourism ecosystem, face great challenges caused by disruptive forces and recently emerged digital players such as search engines, social media, online travel agencies or sharing economy platforms (Gretzel et al. 2015). Due to changing circumstances, DMOs are in search of a new model and their main role in a destination network. The traditional roles of DMOs in marketing communication and product development are being questioned. Based on qualitative research, Dredge, Phi, Mahadevan, Meehan, and Popescu (2018) state that the role of DMOs should shift toward capacity-building roles. DMO representatives highlighted that DMOs have an important role in creating the collaborative environment and preparing and nurturing the spaces of engagement, education and consultation in the destination environment. Therefore, the role of DMO as a leader in knowledge transfer in a destination is gaining importance. However, so far, this radical shift has been analysed only qualitatively. In order to proceed further and find the role of a DMO in a destination network, the combination of quantitative and qualitative analysis with the help of network science approach can bring more light to this problem.

In order to quantitatively examine the role of DMOs in a destination network, social network analysis is performed on two networks in one mature destination, the High Tatras. This destination was chosen for two reasons. Firstly, it is a representative of traditional recreational destinations, offering a purely tourism-based perspective compared to urban destinations. Recreational destinations are viable options to decongest many times overcrowded global urban destinations and reduce the pressure on their resources. Thus, smart tourism

DOI: 10.4324/9781003269342-7

initiatives will need to focus more on the regional approach (Gretzel 2018) and less focus on so far dominated smart city approach (Coca-Stefaniak & Seisdedos 2021). Secondly, this destination was chosen based on its international significance and its long tradition in tourism development. This destination has been during the last two centuries a place of winter sport and health tourism. It is a mature destination with an established governance structure. It can be regarded as a representative of a typical European destination, as the majority of tourism destinations in Europe have a community-based structure and due to the long development of tourism in these destinations, they are in the mature stage of destination lifecycle. Mature destinations have the ability to implement smart initiatives, as smartness is viewed as a step further in destination management (UNWTO 2019). Moreover, from the demand perspective, it has the ability to focus not only on the domestic but also on the international tourism market (Kvasnová et al. 2019). Thus, this destination can serve as a representative of a typical European destination on its way to smartness. The networks will be examined with selected quantitative characteristics of network analysis.

4.1 The role of destination management organisation in a network based on cooperation in marketing activities

DMOs operate in a highly networked marketing environment characterised by a wide variety of stakeholders. In order to achieve organisational success, DMO marketing activities should consider all such stakeholders in a destination (Line & Wang 2017). In order to quantitatively examine the role of DMO, firstly, the stakeholders in the destination have to be identified. The current tourism stakeholders in the destination were identified based on the lists provided by the DMO, local tourism associations and the destination management system (information system). As local tourism associations should have the best knowledge of destination stakeholders and destination management system is used to provide information to visitors on attractions and services, it can be assumed that the number of identified 153 stakeholders comes close to the actual number of current stakeholders in the High Tatras. These stakeholders include DMO, tourism association, accommodation and catering facilities, sport and recreational facilities, spa facilities, cultural facilities, transport associations, municipalities and travel agencies (Table 4.1).

The beginning of formalised cooperative behaviour of destination stakeholders in the High Tatras started in 1994 with the creation of the

Table 4.1 Structure of tourism stakeholders in the destination High Tatras

Category of Stakeholder	No.	Percentage (%)
Tourism organisations	3	1.96%
Accommodation facility	107	69.93%
Catering facility	15	9.80%
Sport and recreational facility	5	3.27%
Cultural facility	3	1.96%
Transport company	2	1.31%
Travel agency	10	6.54%
Spa facility	5	3.27%
Municipality	3	1.96%

Tourism Association of the High Tatras, which represents the interest of accommodation and catering facilities. Although this association created the baseline for cooperation, it was the creation of the DMO Region High Tatras in 2012 that started the application of cooperative destination management. The mission of the DMO is to increase the competitiveness and attractiveness of the destination High Tatras in the domestic and international tourism market and to create the brand and image of the destination. This DMO represents the interest of three municipalities (Vysoké Tatry, Poprad and Štrba), the Tourism Association of the High Tatras, the operators of mountain transport facilities (TMR) and aqua park. Tourism businesses (e.g. accommodation and catering facilities, travel agencies, sport and recreational facilities) are represented by the Tourism Association.

The level of cooperation of destination stakeholders was identified based on the relationships during the creation of a complex tourism product, its distribution and integrated marketing communication of a destination. Secondary sources of information were used regarding destination brochures, internal materials of destination management organisation and destination management system. The relations were identified on a binary basis, not taking into account the intensity of cooperation and were proceeded by network analysis. In this case, the matrix of a network is symmetric and binary, has the shape of a square and contains variables with values '0' and '1'. The rows and columns in the matrix represent the stakeholders, while the individual binary values show whether these subjects cooperate or not (0 = stakeholders do not cooperate, 1 = stakeholders cooperate) (Figure 4.1).

Based on these criteria, the matrix of destination stakeholders and their relationships in marketing activities in the High Tatras in the year 2020 was created and proceeded by network analysis. It can be assumed

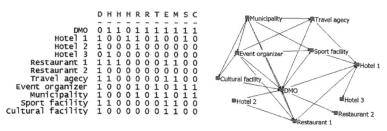

	D	H	H	H	R	R	T	E	M	S	C
DMO	0	1	1	0	1	1	1	1	1	1	1
Hotel 1	1	0	0	1	1	0	1	0	0	1	0
Hotel 2	1	0	0	0	1	0	0	0	0	0	0
Hotel 3	0	1	0	0	0	0	0	0	0	0	0
Restaurant 1	1	1	1	0	0	0	0	1	1	0	0
Restaurant 2	1	0	0	0	0	0	0	0	0	0	0
Travel agency	1	1	0	0	0	0	0	1	1	0	0
Event organizer	1	0	0	0	1	0	1	0	1	1	1
Municipality	1	0	0	0	1	0	1	1	0	1	1
Sport facility	1	1	0	0	0	0	0	1	1	0	0
Cultural facility	1	0	0	0	0	0	0	1	1	0	0

Figure 4.1 Example of a binary matrix and undirected graph of network analysis.

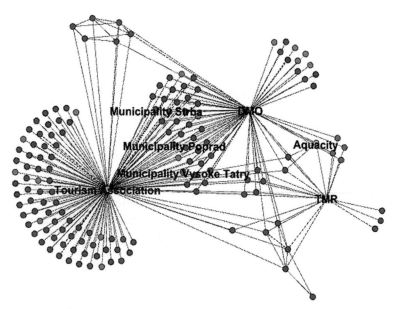

Figure 4.2 Graph of the network based on cooperation in marketing activities in the destination High Tatras.

that such a network based on these criteria comes close to the actual network of stakeholders' relations in the destination (Figure 4.2).

The graph of this network in the High Tatras indicates that the cooperation of stakeholders in marketing activities is concentrated in the Tourism Association. The second most important subject is the DMO. The private stakeholder TMR, Inc., also has an important position in the cooperative behaviour. Besides the graphical

Table 4.2 Quantitative characteristics of network based on cooperation in marketing activities in the High Tatras

Metric	year 2015	year 2020	Typical Destination
Density	0.018	0.020	0.027
Average path length	2.221	2.167	3.389
Clustering coefficient	0.543	0.847	0.201
Global efficiency	0.45	0.46	0.249

Source: Baggio 2020; Gajdošík 2015 and own elaboration.

interpretation, the quantitative characteristics of network analysis give more precise information on the network and enable comparison (Table 4.2).

Thanks to previous research in 2015 based on the same criteria of identification of stakeholders and their cooperation (Gajdošík 2015), it is possible to compare the situation in the analysed destination in time. Moreover, the research of Baggio (2020) provides the outline of network characteristics of a 'typical destination'. This research summarises the main global characteristics of networks by averaging the values of seven destination-based networks (Western Australia, city of Cremona – Italy, island of Elba – Italy, the region of Costa Smeralda-Gallura – Italy, the Golden Coast region – Australia, the city of Livigno – Italy and Sibiu county – Romania) and four destination networks based on the web presence of different destination stakeholders (the tourism web space of Austria, the tourism web space of the Fiji Islands, tourism websites of the Halland County – Sweden and tourism web space of Western Australia).

Comparing the characteristics in time reveals that the network based on cooperation in marketing activities in the High Tatras has become stronger during the examined five years. The density, as the ratio between the total number of links and the maximum number of links that a network can have, is slightly higher. The average path length is getting shorter (2.167 in 2020 compared to 2.221 in 2015). In 2015, stakeholders in the questionnaire survey claimed that cooperation has several barriers. The most important were the lack of trust, lack of contact and the fear of misusing the cooperation. These barriers have been only slightly disappearing, as the clustering coefficient, measured as a probability that a subject cooperates with another subject in the network, indicates that the level of cooperation in marketing activities among destination stakeholders is only slightly increasing. However, the presented situation creates a more efficient network, where the global efficiency of the network is rising.

When comparing the situation in 2020 with the typical destination, the network in the High Tatras has comparable density and better characteristics of average path length, clustering coefficient and global efficiency. On the one hand, it can be the result of strong activities of all stakeholders in this area. On the other hand, the average values creating the typical destination are based on networks representing larger destinations (regional and national) with much more stakeholders taken into account ($\bar{x}$ = 858,36). These global network characteristics give valuable information about the network topologies and are the baseline for the in-depth analysis of the networks.

In order to examine the role of the DMO in the network, the characteristics of node centrality are important. Many network researchers have identified the impact of the central position of actors in the network (e.g. Abdel-Ghany 2012; Balkundi & Kilduff 2005; Borgatti 2006). Actors who have the central position are more active, have shorter paths and have more ties with other members of the network. Centrality measures are important indicators pointing to privileged positions of some stakeholders compared to other members of the network. This special privilege is attributed only in relative terms, as there is no absolute value to indicate high vs. low privilege (Todeva 2006). The privileged actors are bridges between other actors and other stakeholders have to go through them in order to reach other stakeholders in the network. The most commonly used centrality measures are degree centrality, betweenness centrality, closeness centrality and eigenvector centrality.

Network centralities (Table 4.3) measure the structural importance of actors and indicate which actor can be regarded as the one on the centre of networks (Borgatti 2006). This position will confer the power. Power is afforded through the number of direct ties an actor has (degree centrality), the extent of independent access to others (closeness centrality) and control over others (betweenness centrality) (Friedman & Miles 2006). The eigenvector centrality measures the overall influence of the actor (Baggio 2020).

Considering degree centrality, the power is based on the stakeholder degree. Stakeholders who have more ties have greater opportunities because they have choices. This autonomy makes them less dependent on any specific stakeholder in the destination, and hence more powerful. In the analysed destination, the highest degree has the

Table 4.3 Centrality measures based on cooperation in marketing activities in the destination High Tatras

Organisation	Degree	Closeness	Betweenness	Eigenvector	Importance Index
Tourism Association	131	0.859	0.818	1.000	3.097
DMO	72	0.647	0.272	0.642	1.689
TMR	25	0.422	0.046	0.205	0.562
Grand Hotel Stary Smokovec	8	0.512	0.010	0.174	0.291
Grand Hotel Praha	7	0.490	0.007	0.129	0.236
Hotel FIS	5	0.508	0.002	0.161	0.169

Tourism Association. DMO has almost half of the relations with stakeholders compared to the Tourism Association. However, the private actor – TMR, Inc. is slightly gaining power having the degree centrality of 25 in the year 2020, while in 2015 it has the degree of 19 (Gajdošík et al. 2017). It is mainly due to the interdependency between TMR, Inc. and several hotels, restaurants, sports and recreational facilities based on ownership (Figure 4.3).

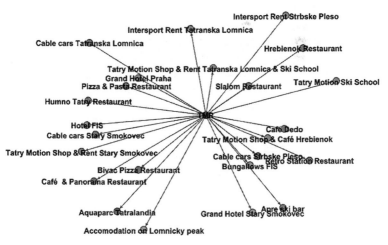

Figure 4.3 Interdependences between TMR, Inc. and other stakeholders based on ownership.

The second reason why a stakeholder can be more powerful than the other stakeholder in the network is that one stakeholder is closer to more stakeholders than any other stakeholder, which is measured by closeness centrality. Power can be exerted through direct bargaining and exchange. But power also comes from acting as a reference point by which other stakeholders judge themselves, and by being the centre of attention. In the High Tatras, the private stakeholders – TMR, Inc. and three hotels have comparable closeness centrality with the DMO. The third reason that a stakeholder is advantaged in the network is because it lies between other pairs of stakeholders and no other stakeholder lies between it and the other stakeholder. The most important players in this sense are Tourism Association, DMO and TMR, Inc.

In order to access the overall importance of stakeholders in the network, the geometric mean of normalised values of degree, closeness, betweenness and eigenvector centrality was calculated and presented as the importance index. Based on this index, it can be concluded that the hubs in the network are tourism organisations (Tourism Association, DMO – public–private bodies) and private bodies (TMR and hotels). DMO does not have the leading position in the network based on cooperation in marketing activities. These results support the research of Beritelli and Laesser (2019), who claim that the activities of DMOs in the marketing of a destination are questionable. To support this research, a primary survey among 329 tourists in Slovakia was conducted. Tourists were asked to name the most important source of awareness of the last destination they visited (Figure 4.4).

The results support the fact that DMOs do not bring guests to the destination, as word of mouth (WOM-family and friends and eWOM – social media, search engines) has higher power compared to the official marketing of a destination (destination website, destination leaflet, official video). DMOs with traditional approaches lose control over the ability to reach and attract tourists. A personalised approach to tourists, which minimises the influence of external intermediaries offering a standardised product, is needed. In the smart tourism ecosystem, DMOs should be able to influence the internal environment of the destination and provide tourists with a personalised experience. In this sense, a new role of the DMO should be analysed, concerning the knowledge transfer among the core stakeholders.

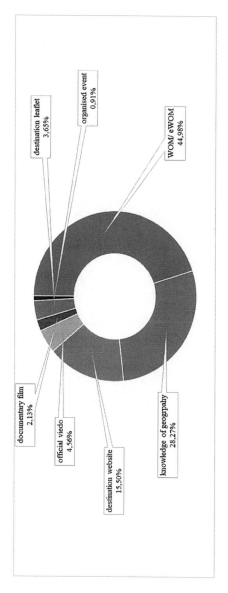

destination leaflet
3.65%

organised event
0.91%

WOM/ eWOM
44.98%

documentary film
2.13%

official viedo
4.56%

destination website
15.50%

knowledge of geogrpahy
28.27%

Figure 4.4 The source of awareness of a destination.

4.2   The role of destination management organisation in a network based on knowledge transfer

The strategic aim of a tourism destination is to be competitive while ensuring sustainable management of resources. In this sense, innovation is needed, where effective knowledge transfer is the prerequisite for innovation (Raisi et al. 2020). Only a few studies have empirically examined the network perspective of knowledge transfer in a destination (Del Chiappa & Baggio 2015; Raisi et al. 2020), however, they did not focus specifically on the role of DMO in this kind of network. Therefore, further analysis is focused on the examination of the role of DMO in the network based on knowledge transfer.

In order to identify the knowledge transfer, the technological virtual network was used. The rationale for using the technological virtual network is twofold. Firstly, ICTs have radically changed the way in which information is conveyed throughout the industry and to customers. The Internet (websites, applications and services) provides a wide availability of data, thus allowing to gather the material useful for creating complex networks (Scott et al. 2008). Secondly, virtual networks can potentially mirror and represent real networks (Baggio & Del Chiappa 2014) and are less costly to study (Raisi et al. 2018). The use of virtual networks also represents a smart way of collecting and analysing data, thus strengthening the smart approach to destination governance.

The directed and weighted network was chosen in order to better represent the flow of information among stakeholders. In this case, the adjacency matrix is non-binary and asymmetric (Figure 4.5). The non-binary values represent the amount of information transferred through the links, while the asymmetricity focuses on the direction (in or out from a node) of the information.

The network based on knowledge transfer was created in the destination High Tatras, using the Webometric Analyst application (Thelwall 2018). Firstly, the knowledge transfer was examined based on URL citations using the search engine Google. The URL citation represents the URL mention on a website in the form of a hyperlink or URL mention. Due to the limit of the search engine, where weighted direct link networks of up to 22 sites can be calculated, the links among the most important stakeholders in the network analysed previously were examined (Figure 4.6). Although this approach is not capable of analysing the whole network of stakeholders, the selection of the most important stakeholders can provide useful results that can be further analysed. The aim of this analysis is to find the most

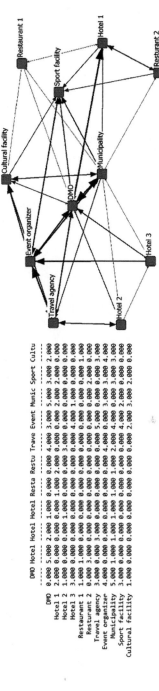

Figure 4.5 Example of a weighted matrix and directed graph of network analysis.

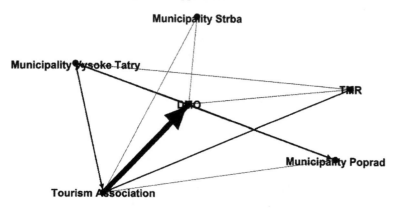

Figure 4.6 Graph of the network based on knowledge transfer of the most important stakeholders in the destination High Tatras.

important stakeholders that gather knowledge and are capable of spreading it to other stakeholders.

Following the graphical interpretation of the knowledge transfer network, the most important link is between the Tourism Association and the DMO. The reason for the strength is the direct connection through the application programming interface (API). Tourism Association produces open data, which are implemented through API in the website of DMO. Therefore, the knowledge is transferred from the Tourism Association to the DMO. Knowledge transfer among other stakeholders is significantly lower. This situation is also supported using centrality measures of the network analysis (Table 4.4).

Table 4.4 Centrality measures based on knowledge transfer in the destination High Tatras

Organisation	In-degree	Closeness	Betweenness	Left-Eigenvector	Importance Index
DMO	1976	0.571	0.708	0.847	5.101
Tourism Association	887	0.667	0.750	1.000	4.590
Municipality Vysoke Tatry	647	0.800	0.875	0.590	4.043
Municipality Poprad	436	0.800	0.875	0.280	3.040
Municipality Strba	13	0.500	0.853	0.400	1.220

For directed weighted networks, the previously used centrality measures have to be modified. To calculate the 'prestige' of a node, in-degree centrality counting the number of incoming ties is used. Closeness centrality is not well suited to directed data in fragmented networks. However, the network based on knowledge transfer in the High Tatras is not fragmented, therefore the use of closeness centrality is appropriate. Betweenness centrality can be applied to directed data without any modification. The eigenvector is similar to degree centrality, where the eigenvector centrality can be split into two concepts – the right eigenvector corresponding to out-degree and the left eigenvector corresponding to in-degree. In this case, the use of the left eigenvector is used to indicate the amount of direct and indirect potential influence of the node (Borgatti et al. 2018). Based on the geometric mean of these centrality measures, the importance index was calculated.

As the differences in importance index are not statistically significant, multi-dimensional scaling (MDS) is used to prove the position of the analysed stakeholders. This multivariate statistical technique positions the network nodes in the way that interconnected nodes are close together. MDS places nodes in a space such that the distances between points correspond in a predetermined way to the proximities among nodes (Borgatti et al. 2018). The graphical output of MDS shows trends and clusters more clearly than the network graph (Figure 4.7).

The proximities in MDS were regarded as similarities, so the nodes with the highest values are near each other on the map. When building the proximity matrix, the Pearson correlation as proximity measure was used. This matrix was further proceeded by metric MDS used for weighted data. The MDS was calculated with the amount of distortion, known as 'stress', of 0.188. Following the recommendation of Borgatti, Everett, and Johnson (2018), who consider the stress values of less than 0.2 to be acceptable when using metric MDS, we consider the outcomes of MDS useful for this study.

To find the clusters of stakeholders that are closer to each other, the hierarchical agglomerative clustering based on proximity matrix and average linkage algorithm was used. Agglomerative clustering starts with each object representing an individual cluster. The objects are then sequentially merged to form clusters of multiple objects, starting with the two most similar objects, where similarity is defined in terms of distance between objects. The average linkage algorithm sets the distance between two clusters as the average distance between all pairs of cluster members. Agglomerative clustering thus establishes a

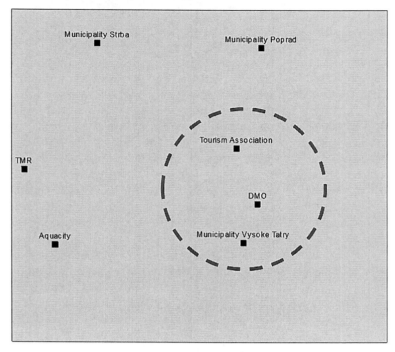

Figure 4.7 Graphical output of MDS on the network based on knowledge
transfer in the destination High Tatras.

hierarchy of objects from the bottom to the top (Sarstedt & Mooi
2019). The graphical output of the hierarchical clustering is the dendrogram (Figure 4.8).

To specify the number of clusters, the dendrogram is cut vertically, where no merger occurred for a long distance. In our case, the
cluster analysis indicated a four-cluster solution. Following the
results of MDS and cluster analysis, it can be stated that the most
important stakeholders in gathering the knowledge are DMO,
Tourism Association and municipality Vysoké Tatry. The reason for
the creation of this cluster is the connection of their websites through
API. When there is a new information (e.g. new event in the destination), an organiser or employee of the Tourism Association fills in
the predefined form. Further, the information is proceeded in a
machine-readable format and stored in a cloud as an open data. In
this case, DMO recognises its position as an information hub and
uses the API to access and gather data.

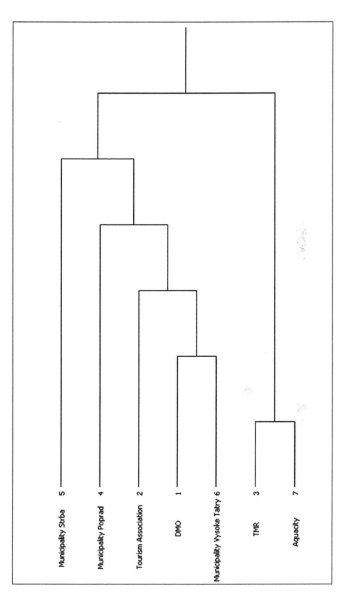

Figure 4.8 Dendrogram of hierarchical agglomerative clustering based on proximity matrix of knowledge transfer in the destination High Tatras.

However, for effective knowledge transfer, collecting the data is not sufficient. It is also important to spread the knowledge to the internal and external stakeholders. In this way, websites, social media and newsletters are the most important channels (Morrison 2019). As from the methodological point of view, it is difficult to analyse large networks of website URL mentions, the analysis of knowledge spread is done using data from newsletters. For this analysis, only the most important stakeholders based on knowledge gathering were used – the DMO and the Tourism Association. These organisations use an automatic mail program to inform the internal and external stakeholders. The databases of e-mail contacts, where regular newsletters concerning the destination development are sent, were accessed. Together, 354 contacts on stakeholders were found in the database of DMO and 216 contacts in the database of the Tourism Association. As the Tourism Association is strongly cooperating with the DMO in informing stakeholders, the majority of stakeholders are in the databases of both organisations. However, the DMO has more links to external destination stakeholders. Thus, DMO has a stronger position in spreading the information to stakeholders. Moreover, it is often due to the link to external organisations producing new knowledge that is believed to improve innovation and competitive advantage (Raisi et al. 2020).

In this way, DMO is considered rightly a hub, where knowledge is gathered and subsequently spread among stakeholders. Therefore, the most important stakeholder in knowledge transfer is the DMO, that is, managing this network and has a structural position as a hub. Following the research of Dhanaraj and Parkhe (2006), hubs orchestrate network activities to ensure the creation and extraction of value. Orchestration comprises knowledge mobility, innovation appropriability and network stability. Other organisations may play similar roles but possess other positions in the networks, for example, as 'superstructure organisations' providing collective goods and coordinating information flows (Sørensen & Balsby 2021). This is the case of the Tourism Association, which provides open data for general use for other organisations.

This analysis proved that in the smart tourism ecosystem, DMO has the ability to be the leader in knowledge transfer, clearly establishing the leading role in this kind of network. This structural position in the network quantitatively proves the outcome of qualitative research of Femenia-Serra and Ivars-Baidal (2019), who studied the opinions of destination managers on the effect of the smart tourism ecosystem on destination management organisations. However, as Del Chiappa and Baggio (2015) emphasise, many other factors may influence the ability to exchange knowledge. Therefore, there is a need for a deeper empirical understanding of specific factors that influence the process of information sharing a consensus development among stakeholders. In this regard, the analysis of smart business ecosystem is needed.

4.3 Destination management organisation as a data hub in the smart ecosystem

The analysis of DMO's role in smart tourism ecosystem revealed that DMOs are becoming the leaders in the network of knowledge transfer. However, the structural characteristics of the examined networks have not taken into account the ability or willingness of stakeholders to share the information. To proceed further, more in-depth research was conducted among tourism businesses. Together, 114 hospitality facilities, 34 travel agencies, 39 cultural facilities and 21 sport and recreation facilities were analysed using semi-structured interviews held in 2020 and 2021 in Slovakia. These businesses were asked to give their opinion on their willingness to share data with other stakeholders in a destination.

As the sources of data collection vary, the owners of the data are also different. Search engines collect their own dynamic data on Internet searches, reservation system providers (e.g. Booking.com, Expedia) have their own booking and searching databases, mobile operators store their own location data and also destination stakeholders (e.g. hotels, travel agencies, sport and recreational facilities, cultural facilities) use their own databases. Moreover, the sensors embedded in destination environments have many times their own owners (e.g. retail shops, police). Therefore, the willingness to share data is crucial. From the answers of the analysed businesses, the network concerning the willingness to share data with other stakeholders was created (Figure 4.9).

The network is directed and weighted according to the level of willingness ranging from very unwilling to very willing. From the graphical representation, it is evident that the DMO and the event organisers are stakeholders with which other stakeholders are the most willing to share data. The DMO has the highest in-degree centrality, showing that this organisation is considered a knowledge hub among tourism businesses.

The created network mirrors the smart business ecosystem, which is considered an inherent part of the smart tourism ecosystem. This ecosystem creates an environment with established relationships between stakeholders determining interaction and knowledge sharing (Baggio & Del Chiappa 2013). Within this ecosystem, social capital between tourism businesses is created contributing to trust, lower

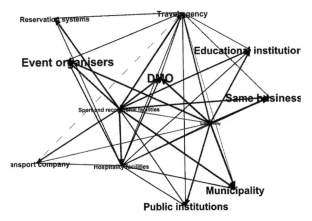

Figure 4.9 Network concerning the willingness to share data with other stakeholders.

transaction costs and leading to increased willingness to share knowledge (Bachinger et al. 2020). These factors favour the transfer of tacit knowledge in a destination, which is very difficult to replicate and purchase. Moreover, such a knowledge is difficult to access to members outside the ecosystem, therefore strengthening the competitive position of a destination. In this way, the role of a DMO should shift to inter-stakeholder management and knowledge sharing and focus less on marketing activities (Figure 4.10).

The smart tourism ecosystem creates tougher conditions, where the destination is challenged with higher dynamics and uncertainty.

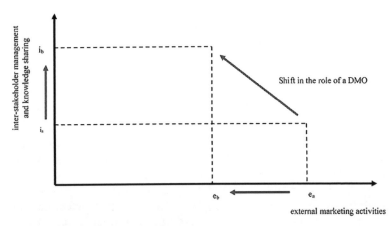

Figure 4.10 Shifting the role of a DMO.

Gretzel (2022) identified six roles of smart DMOs, namely: mobilising, match-making, managing, sensing, shapeshifting and stewardship. These roles are built on the need of open innovation, data observatories, real-time monitoring and free flow of data and human capital. Therefore, in order to design unique tourism experiences, it is essential that the DMO is able to use the data collected in order to provide solutions that satisfy destination stakeholders. Thus, DMOs should also become data mining organisations, where the knowledge is significantly enhanced by applying the methods of Business Intelligence. Knowledge activities should deal with extracting information from different customer- and supplier-based sources, as well as with the generation of relevant knowledge which can be applied in the form of intelligent services for customers and stakeholders (Fuchs et al. 2014).

Business intelligence opens the door to opportunities to handle complex, unstructured data from multiple data sources and emphasise the analytical process of turning data into actionable strategies for better decisions (Vajirakachorn & Chongwatpol 2017). Therefore, in order to govern destinations in a smart way, a technological platform built on state-of-the-art technologies managing and centralising the data from stakeholders and ensuring a real-time access is needed.

To summarise the analysis of the role of a DMO in the smart tourism ecosystem, it can be stated that the role of DMO is changing. Inter-stakeholder management and knowledge sharing are becoming the vital roles of DMOs in the smart tourism ecosystem, leaving marketing at a lower level among priorities. DMOs are becoming knowledge hubs where data mining approaches strengthen the competitiveness of a destination. Technology offers valuable tools for collaboration, thereby enhancing the potential for knowledge sharing. With smart technologies, knowledge and information are accessible to all stakeholders, thus increasing the innovation potential and competitiveness of a destination (Pesonen 2020). Thus, DMOs should transform themselves into knowledge keepers and supporters of information spread, having advisory roles in planning and designing public spaces, provided that they also have an overview of what the visitors are doing and can assess this together with the actors in the destination (Beritelli & Laesser 2019).

References

Abdel-Ghany, M., 2012. Identifying opinion leaders using social network analysis, a study in an Egyptian village. *Russian Journal of Agricultural and Socio-Economic Sciences*, 4 (4), 12–19.

Bachinger, M., Kofler, I., and Pechlaner, H., 2020. Sustainable instead of high-growth? Entrepreneurial ecosystems in tourism. *Journal of Hospitality and Tourism Management*, 44 (July), 238–242.

Baggio, R., 2020. Tourism destinations: A universality conjecture based on network science. *Annals of Tourism Research*, 82 (April), 102929.

Baggio, R., and Del Chiappa, G., 2013. Tourism destinations as digital business ecosystems. *In*: Cantoni L, and Xiang Z, eds. *Information and communication technologies in tourism 2013*. Berlin: Springer.

Baggio, R., and Del Chiappa, G., 2014. Real and virtual relationships in tourism digital ecosystems. *Information Technology and Tourism*, 14 (1), 3–19.

Balkundi, P., and Kilduff, M., 2005. The ties that lead: A social network approach to leadership. *The Leadership Quarterly*, 16 (6), 941–961.

Beritelli, P., and Laesser, C., 2019. Warum DMOs und tourismusorganisationen nicht wirklich 'Gäste holen' - Die Aufklärung eines cargo-kults. *In*: *Schweizer jahrbuch für tourismus. Neue technologien und kommunikation im alpinen tourismus*. Berlin: Erich Schmidt Verlag GmbH & Co KG, 53–83.

Borgatti, S., Everett, M., and Johnson, J., 2018. *Analysing social networks*. 2nd edition London: SAGE Publications.

Borgatti, S.P., 2006. Identifying sets of key players in a social network. *Computational and Mathematical Organization Theory*, 12 (1), 21–34.

Coca-Stefaniak, J., and Seisdedos, G., 2021. Smart urban tourism destinations at a crossroads. *In*: A. Morrison, and J. Coca-Stefaniak, eds. *Routledge handbook of tourism cities*. Oxon: Routledge, 359–373.

Del Chiappa, G., and Baggio, R., 2015. Knowledge transfer in smart tourism destinations: Analyzing the effects of a network structure. *Journal of Destination Marketing and Management*, 4 (3), 143–144.

Dhanaraj, C., and Parkhe, A., 2006. Orchestrating innovation networks. *Academy of Management Review*, 31 (3), 659–669

Dredge, D., Phi, G., Mahadevan, R., Meehan, E., and Popescu, E., 2018. *Digitalisation in tourism. In-depth analysis of challenges and opportunities*. Copenhagen: Aalborg University

Femenia-Serra, F., and Ivars-Baidal, J.A., 2019. DMOs: Surviving the smart tourism ecosystem. *In*: Buhalis, D., ed. *Travel and tourism research association conference*. Bournemouth: Bournemouth University, 1–3.

Friedman, A., and Miles, S., 2006. *Stakeholders: Theory and practice*. Oxford: Oxford University Press.

Fuchs, M., Höpken, W., and Lexhagen, M., 2014. Big data analytics for knowledge generation in tourism destinations – A case from Sweden. *Journal of Destination Marketing & Management*, 3 (4), 198–209.

Gajdošík, T., 2015. Network analysis of cooperation in tourism destinations. *Czech Journal of Tourism*, 4 (1), 26–44.

Gajdošík, T., Gajdošíková, Z., Maráková, V., and Flagestad, A., 2017. Destination structure revisited in view of the community and corporate model. *Tourism Management Perspectives*, 24 (October), 54–63.

Gretzel, U., 2018. From smart destinations to smart tourism regions. *Investigaciones Regionales*, 2018 (42), 171–184.

Gretzel, U., 2022. The smart DMO: A new step in the digital transformation of destination management organizations. *European Journal of Tourism Research*, 30 (2022), 3002–3002.

Gretzel, U., Werthner, H., Koo, C., and Lamsfus, C., 2015. Conceptual foundations for understanding smart tourism ecosystems. *Computers in Human Behavior*, 50, 558–563.

Kvasnová, D., Gajdošík, T., and Maráková, V., 2019. Are partnerships enhancing tourism destination competitiveness? *Acta Universitatis Agriculturae et Silviculturae Mendelianae Brunensis*, 67 (3), 811–821.

Line, N.D., and Wang, Y., 2017. Market-oriented destination marketing. *Journal of Travel Research*, 56 (1), 122–135.

Morrison, A.M., 2019. *Marketing and managing tourism destinations*. Oxon: Routledge.

Pesonen, J., 2020. Management and leadership for digital transformation in tourism. *In*: Z. Xiang, M. Fuchs, U. Gretzel, and W. Höpken, eds. *Handbook of e-tourism*. Cham: Springer International Publishing, 1–34.

Raisi, H., Baggio, R., Barratt-Pugh, L., and Willson, G., 2018. Hyperlink network analysis of a tourism destination. *Journal of Travel Research*, 57 (5), 671–686.

Raisi, H., Baggio, R., Barratt-Pugh, L., and Willson, G., 2020. A network perspective of knowledge transfer in tourism. *Annals of Tourism Research*, 80 (March 2019), 102817.

Sarstedt, M., and Mooi, E., 2019. *A concise guide to market research: The process, data, and methods using IBM SPSS statistics*. 3rd edition Springer-Verlag Berlin Heidelberg.

Scott, N., Baggio, R., and Cooper, C., 2008. *Network analysis and tourism, From theory to practice*. Clevedon: Channel View Publications.

Sørensen, F., and Balsby, N., 2021. Brokers and saboteurs: Actor roles in destination innovation network development. *Tourism Planning & Development*, 18 (5) 547–572.

Thelwall, M., 2018. *Big data and social web research methods*. Wolverhampton: University of Wolverhampton.

Todeva, E., 2006. *Business networks: Strategy and structure*. Oxon: Routledge.

UNWTO, 2019. *UNWTO guidlines for institutional strenghtening of destination management organizations (DMOs). Preparing DMOs for new challenges*. Madrid: UNWTO.

Vajirakachorn, T., and Chongwatpol, J., 2017. Application of business intelligence in the tourism industry: A case study of a local food festival in Thailand. *Tourism Management Perspectives*, 23, 75–86.

5 Data analytics for a dynamic construct of a tourism destination

The third challenge of tourism destination governance is the need to take more into account the intersection of tourism demand and supply in a destination. The traditional administrative model of a destination is often an obstacle to the development of tourism in terms of limiting boundaries and emphasising the supply side of a destination. Therefore, it is appropriate to enrich it with dynamic elements and factors influenced by visitor flows. This dynamic view on destination responds to the current problems of destination management organisations, where stakeholders question the ability of DMOs to attract tourists and influence their travel decision (Reinhold et al. 2019). The economic success of a destination depends on multiple flows whose prospects need to be governed in the mid to long term (Beritelli et al. 2019). Understanding visitor flows enables destination managers and stakeholders to smartly create tourism experiences and include a demand-driven approach in the process (Cvelbar et al. 2018).

The dynamic construct of a destination requires a large amount of data to be collected and proceed. In this way, the smart approach combining transdisciplinary approaches by taking into account the advanced data analytics and the design perspective could be useful. Technology can help to collect and analyse the data. Although Beritelli, Reinhold, and Laesser (2020) argue that existing IT-based instruments to collect visitor data and algorithmic methods to analyse them still cannot fully explain and predict the drivers of visitor behaviour, the chapter analyses the importance of smart approach in finding the intersection of demand and supply in a destination.

DOI: 10.4324/9781003269342-8

5.1 Identifying strategic visitor flows using big data analytics

Visitor flows can be identified using traditional techniques (Beritelli & Laesser 2017; Hwang, Gretzel, & Fesenmaier 2006; Shih 2006). These traditional techniques, using surveys and travel diaries, represent the so-called 'small data'. Small data are characterised by their limited volume, non-continuous collection, narrow variety, and are usually generated to answer specific questions (Kitchin & Lauriault 2015). Small data are static, changing occasionally or are aggregated at coarse timescale (month, quarter, year) (Ricciato et al. 2020). Therefore, they are not always suitable as they provide past static data and their collection is often time-consuming and misleading. Unlike small data, big data refers to large growing datasets that include heterogeneous formats and has a complex nature that requires powerful technologies and advanced algorithms (Oussous et al. 2018). In order to find strategic visitor flows, the use of big data is welcomed, which can include information from mobile positing, destination smart cards or geotagged information from social media. The strengths and weaknesses of the most used traditional and big data techniques in analysing visitor flows are summarised in Table 5.1.

Table 5.1 The most used techniques to analyse visitor flows

Technique	Strengths	Weaknesses
Survey	ability to analyse in-depth characteristics (e.g. motives, satisfaction)	time-consuming, difficult to have a representative sample
Travel diary	precise data	time-consuming, difficult to have a representative sample
GPS	precise data, possibility to analyse movement	small sample, possible changes in behaviour when being monitored
Smart cards	data on consumption	difficult to have a representative sample
Mobile application	big sample, possibility to analyse movement	difficult to have a representative sample, dependent on a third party
Social media	big sample, inexpensive, ability to analyse in-depth characteristics (e.g. gender, preferences), possibility to analyse movement	difficult to have a representative sample
Passive mobile positioning	big sample, possibility to analyse movement	expensive

The GPS technique is challenged with small sample sizes, while when using smart cards, mobile applications or social media to analyse visitor flows, it is very hard to achieve the representativeness of the sample, as not all types of tourists use these technologies. On the other hand, social media enables monitoring spatial, temporal and demographic characteristics as well as the movement of tourists. Moreover, mobile positioning helps to obtain comprehensive paths of tourists in spatial and temporal facets from a large sample of mobile users (Park & Zhong 2021).

Thanks to the available data based on smart approach, DMOs and destination stakeholders should have a clear picture of the tourist mobility in and near the destination. Data can be further examined in order to find out the geographical segmentation of flows, most visited attractions and thus to determine tourism zones and boundaries of a destination.

In order to show the contribution of the smart approach to the identification of visitor flows, the data from passive mobile positioning in the destination High Tatras was used. Passive mobile positioning can be viewed as an efficient tool to strategically analyse tourist flows (Baggio & Scaglione 2018). From a methodological point of view, the distinction between residents and tourists was made based on 'sleeping locality'. Those SIM cards that were logged regularly in the area were treated as residential and were excluded from further research. Due to high costs, other filters (e.g. geographical location of tourists) were not applied.

The first result of passive mobile positioning was a time series of the number of tourists for the date range of 119 days. However, the linear approach to time series analysis did not provide the expected outcome, as the identification of cycles is, due to the complexity and short period, questionable. As tourism destinations are viewed as complex dynamic systems, specific methods and tools are required in the analysis to better tailor governance and policy measures (Baggio 2013). Understanding the complexity features, the non-linear approaches to the analysis of time series are welcomed with the help of network analysis (Baggio & Sainaghi 2016). In order to transform time series into networks, the horizontal visibility graph (HVG) algorithm is a useful approach. The HVG is a methodology that transforms a time series into a graph, maintaining the inherent characteristics of the transformed time series. It considers each point in the time series a node in the network connected by the following consideration: Let $\{x_i, i = 1, ..., N\}$, be a time series of N data. Two nodes i and j in the graph are connected if it is possible to trace a horizontal line, in the time series, linking x_i and x_j not intersecting the intermediate data height, fulfilling: $x_i, x_j > x_n$ for all $i < n < j$ (Gonçalves et al. 2016).

The available data from mobile positioning in the high Tatras provides time series of the number of tourists from 16 December 2019 to 12 April 2020. These daily data can be a complement to traditional accommodation statistics available on a monthly basis. Moreover, it can better access the volatility and quick changes in the behaviour of visitor flows. This can be done by finding the turning points in the time series using the modularity analysis. Modularity analysis uses community detection to create communities (subgroups of nodes) within the network (Borgatti et al. 2018). Nodes belonging to the same community represent periods with the same economic dynamics. Modularity analysis makes it possible to reveal these different periods and identify various phases (Baggio & Sainaghi 2016). In the destination context, it is the dynamics of visitor flows and turning points in their behaviour.

In order to identify the touring points in tourist behaviour in the High Tatras, the modularity analysis was performed on the identified time series. The modularity index of the network $Q = 0.781$ indicates a good separation between different nodes. The analysis divided the time series into 10 different dynamic phases (Figure 5.1).

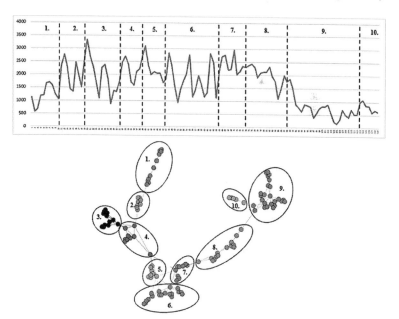

Figure 5.1 Modularity analysis of time series and identification of turning points in visitor behaviour in the High Tatras.

After an in-depth analysis of these phases, there are several interesting implications.

The first phase corresponds to the pre-seasonal behaviour of tourists. The second phase starts on 24 December and lasts until 2 January, which is in line with the first part of Christmas holidays. The third cycle starts before the national holiday on 6 January and lasts until 12 January, embracing the second part of Christmas holidays. From the fourth to sixth phase, the top seasonal behaviour of tourists is evident, with the peaks during the weekends. The eighth and ninth cycles were caused by the spring holidays. The ninth cycle was influenced by the lockdown caused by the COVID-19 crisis, with little recovery in the tenth phase, due to the Easter holidays.

The most interesting implications are revealed in the seventh and eighth cycles. The seventh phase corresponds to the spring holidays in the Bratislava, Trnava and Nitra regions (western Slovakia). The eighth cycle grouped together the spring holidays of Košice and Prešov region (eastern Slovakia) with Banská Bystrica, Žilina and Trenčín region (central Slovakia). The visitor flows were divided based on geographical location. Based on geographic segmentation, visitors from western Slovakia form one flow, while visitors from central and eastern Slovakia form another flow. This proves the applicability of smart data collection through passive mobile positioning and mapping time series into networks as a powerful tool on how to access the characteristics of visitor flows.

Moreover, when analysing visitor flows, tracking the movement of tourists in a destination is among the high priority. In order to analyse the data, the database including anonymised tourist IDs, time sequence and geographical coordinates has to be created (Table 5.2).

The cellphone tower coordinates (X and Y) are considered as a node in the network, while the movement in time and space between two towers represents the network edges. The sequence of tourist movements can be analysed using all records of cellphone towers with

Table 5.2 Example of database concerning tracking the movement of tourists in a destination

Tourist_ID	Time	Coordinate X	Coordinate Y
258478	24.8.2020-09:12:21	20.057505	49.120370
258478	24.8.2020-10:03:45	20.063271	49.125021
258478	24.8.2020-12:15:50	20.059776	49.129025
...	...	...	...

the same tourist ID. When using big data, due to the large number of tourists, processing such a large volume of data is difficult. Therefore, data mining is a promising tool to handle these data. Among the trajectory data mining techniques, trajectory pattern mining and trajectory classification can provide useful information.

Trajectory pattern mining enables to analyse mobility patterns of moving objects. It helps to find representative paths or common trends among data. In order to have a comprehensive picture of visitor flows, there is a need to group tourists into clusters, as well as to use map-matching algorithms (Li et al. 2010). The density-based spatial clustering of applications with noise (DBSCAN) provides a reasonable clustering technique. Sequential pattern mining algorithm can reveal the most used travel routes in a destination (Figure 5.2).

Moreover, different types of visitors do different things in different places at different times (Beritelli 2019). Therefore, it is worth classifying the visitor flows based on certain attributes. Trajectory classification can be used. These attributes can include, for example, used means of transport-based on speed, or domestic or foreign nationality – based on roaming, length of stay – excursionists or holiday-makers). It can be done using supervised learning approaches, such as Conditional Random Fields classification and Decision Tree classifier.

In order to further analyse the mobility of visitor flows, the network analysis of visitor flows in the destination High Tatras was performed. Together, 105 macro clusters and 17 places were identified representing strategic visitor flows in the destination. Each macro cluster was rewritten into matrix format and then the overall matrix for visitor flows was constructed by merging all the trajectories and proceeded by network analysis. The graphical interpretation of the flows shows the most important trajectories in the destination (Figure 5.3).

These trajectories are essential and can explain the travel patterns of tourists in a destination. Knowledge of the logical sequence of

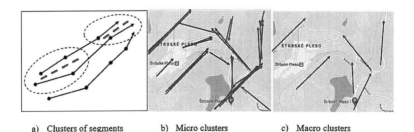

a) Clusters of segments   b) Micro clusters   c) Macro clusters

Figure 5.2 Clustering of visitor flows.

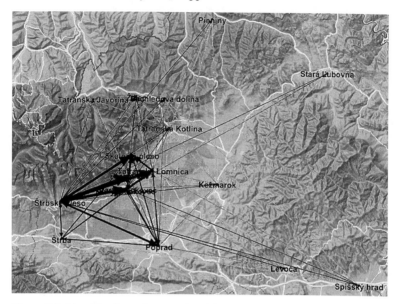

Figure 5.3 Identification of strategic visitor flows in the destination High Tatras.

tourist movement considers spatial dimensions to be essential not only to identify areas for improvement and local strengths, but also to develop strategic destination planning (Park et al. 2020). The most important strength of big data techniques lies in the ability to identify the time-space activities of tourists and the high volume of data enables different statistical approaches with high accuracy. In this way, it can serve to better design destination development and be the starting point for finding the intersection of demand and supply in a destination.

5.2 Finding the intersection between visitor flows and destination stakeholders

The dynamic construct of a destination considers a destination as a space in which visitors perform different sequences of activities in time and space. It is a complex and dynamic ecosystem of exchanges between demand and supply (Beritelli et al. 2020). The success of a destination depends on the action of stakeholders and their ability to attract visitor flows and create synergies for these flows. In this sense, the tourism destination is not a clearly delimited area; its borders are blurry and can only be loosely identified by groups of stakeholders connected by various visitor flows (Beritelli et al. 2019). This is even more important in the smart tourism ecosystem, as due to the large amount of information about a destination and its attractions, tourists move freely in the environment and have more possibilities to explore the area.

In order to construct a destination in a dynamic way, the intersection between visitor flows and destination stakeholders should be made. Therefore, it is inevitable to analyse in depth, the created visitor flows concerning the space of a destination and to find the relevant stakeholders capable of co-creating the experiences for these flows. Following the identification of strategic visitor flows, the structural properties of the network of identified visitor flows in the destination High Tatras were analysed. Based on the recommendation of Asero, Gozzo, and Tomaselli (2016), to explore structural properties of a network created by strategic visitor flows, the most relevant metrics of centrality (in-degree, out-degree and betweenness) are used (Table 5.3).

Table 5.3 Quantitative characteristics of the network of strategic visitor flows in the destination High Tatras

Place	In-Degree	Out-Degree	Betweenness	Strongly Connected Compontent (ID)
Štrbské Pleso	10.0000	16.0000	0.1048	6
Starý Smokovec	9.0000	16.0000	0.0906	6
Nový Smokovec	6.0000	4.0000	0.0008	6
Hrebienok	8.0000	2.0000	0.0000	6
Tatranská Lomnica	9.0000	14.0000	0.0607	6
Skalnaté pleso	8.0000	0.0000	0.0000	6
Tatranská Kotlina	4.0000	11.0000	0.0017	6
Ždiar	5.0000	8.0000	0.0007	6
Tatranská Javorina	4.0000	0.0000	0.0000	5
Poprad	6.0000	16.0000	0.0315	6
Štrba	5.0000	6.0000	0.0031	6
Kežmarok	6.0000	6.0000	0.0019	6
Levoča	4.0000	0.0000	0.0000	3
Spišský hrad	4.0000	6.0000	0.0000	4
Bachledova dolina	8.0000	0.0000	0.0000	2
Pieniny	5.0000	0.0000	0.0000	1
Stará Ľubovňa	4.0000	0.0000	0.0000	0

Concerning visitor flows, in-degree centrality counts the number of incoming flows into a place; therefore, it can be interpreted as a measure of attractiveness or popularity. In the High Tatras, the most attractive places are Štrbské pleso, Starý Smokovec and Tatranská Lomnica. Out-degree centrality counts the number of outgoing flows. Places having the highest out-degree centrality can be considered as departure points. In this case, places such as Štrbské Pleso, Strarý Smokovec and Poprad can be considered as departure points for tourists. Betweenness centrality is calculated as a proportion of all the shortest paths from one place to the other through the focal one. In the context of visitor flows, it indicates the place having the highest influence in the network, as the place is in a critical position between pairs of other places. The most influential places are Štrbské pleso, Starý Smokovec and Tatranská Lomnica. Centrality measures are therefore useful for indicating the role played by places (attractions) in a destination, leading to more sophisticated managerial decisions.

Network analysis can also be used to define the boundaries of a destination. The measure of connected components, where nodes are easily reachable, is useful in this sense. The strongly connected components indicate that there is a path between all pairs of places. Based on the list of strongly connected places, the boundaries can be assigned. In the case of the High Tatras, the destination boundaries should be extended and also include places Tatranská Kotlina, Ždiar and Kežmarok (Figure 5.4).

The in-depth analysis of visitor trajectories, identification of popular departure points, the most influential places and extension of boundaries create opportunities for engaging new destination stakeholders. Since visitors navigate destination space with multiple stakeholders in pursuit of their performance, it is not efficient to optimise the stakeholders and their behaviour. Instead, it is worth engaging as many stakeholders as possible and enhancing the interconnection between several areas in the destination in terms of mobility and information (Beritelli et al. 2020).

The extended destination boundaries indicate the possibility to find new stakeholders. Their virtual presence on the websites of the municipalities and online geographical information systems (Google Maps) concerning the newly identified areas of destination was a prerequisite for their inclusion in the analysis. The analysed network of stakeholders identified on the basis of marketing activities was extended by 39 new stakeholders, including 17 accommodation facilities, nine catering

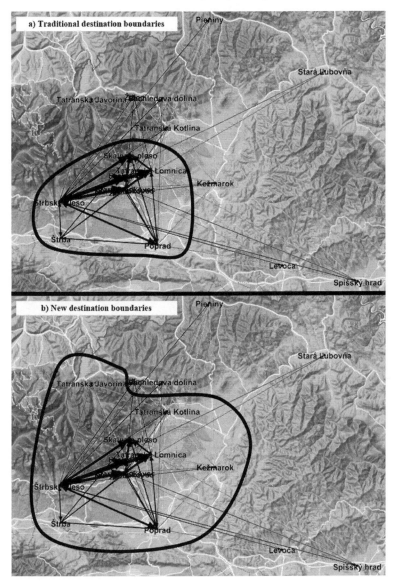

Figure 5.4 Extending destination boundaries based on visitor flows.

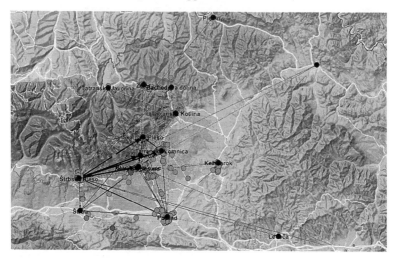

Figure 5.5 Graphical interpretation of the intersection between visitor flows
and destination stakeholders.

facilities, seven cultural facilities, five sports and recreational facilities,
and one spa facility (Figure 5.5).

All these destination stakeholders (traditional and new) should
take the responsibility to attract visitor flows and be able to co-create
the experience with them. All stakeholders should be involved, as each
of them can, directly or indirectly, influence a specific visitor flow. This
data analytic approach enables to find the intersection between
demand and supply of a destination and to find stakeholders that
could have been overlooked and engage them in collaborative design.

5.3 Using the smart approach to get insights into the dynamics of a destination

Greater insights into interrelated visitor flows may provide a practical way to influence the resilience of a tourism destination as a
whole (Koens et al. 2021). The previous analysis revealed that the
identification of the intersection between visitor flows and destination stakeholders based on the smart approach created more precise
and dynamic outcomes compared to traditional techniques of data
collection and analysis. The traditional techniques can be applied to
analyse more in-depth behaviour of tourists (e.g. their motivation,
satisfaction), while the smart approach using big data is useful to
find out the patterns and analyse the movement of tourists within

a destination. Therefore, it should be noted that small data and big data approaches are complementary and should not be treated as substitutes for one another (Duan et al. 2017). The virtual presence of tourism businesses makes it easy to find the intersection between visitor flows and destination stakeholders. Moreover, big data analytics brings more value if network science is used compared to traditional statistical techniques, as it is suitable for dealing with large-scale data.

As the tourism destination is considered as a complex system, the processes in the destination have a dynamic nature. From a network point of view, the dynamic nature of processes that occur in or within a network can significantly influence the destination network. In order to describe and analyse these dynamic processes, system resilience is a useful unit of analysis. The resilience of the network expresses the capacity to withstand internal or external shocks and it is linked to the assortativity of a network. In a complex network, it can be analysed by looking at the changes in structural characteristics of a network when removing certain links or nodes (Baggio 2017).

Assortative networks are dominated by a core group of interconnected high-degree nodes. Such a core group provides robustness to the network. Removing these high-degree nodes is one of the most effective ways to destroy the network connectivity; however, it is less effective because by removing them, the other part of the network is not attacked, thus more resilient. Conversely, in the disassortatively mixed network, removing the high-degree nodes will affect the whole network (Newman 2003).

Assortativity is a common property of social networks. In the case of the analysed destination High Tatras, we compare the assortativity of two networks concerning the traditional and new destination boundaries (Figure 5.6).

Based on the graphical interpretation of the analysed networks, it is evident that in the network concerning new destination boundaries the assortativity is higher. Those places with a similar degree (nodes with similar size) create a core group. The changes in destination boundaries created a more resilient network. For a destination, this generates additional information, helps to exchange know-how and experiences and facilitates the identification of activities relevant to identified visitor flows (Beritelli et al. 2019).

Using the smart approach to get insights into the dynamics of a tourism destination extends the application St. Gallen model of destination management (Beritelli et al. 2013). The model describes that the success of the destination depends on several visitor flows and the ability of stakeholders to reach and manage these flows. For each

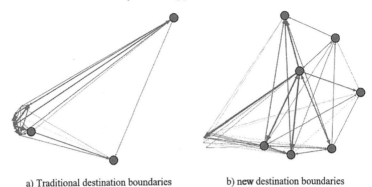

a) Traditional destination boundaries   b) new destination boundaries

Figure 5.6 Assortativity of the networks concerning traditional and new destination boundaries.

visitor flow, it is necessary to define which stakeholders should participate in meeting its needs, what are their managerial and marketing tasks and what initiatives and projects are needed. The smart approach enables greater involvement of stakeholders, who can more easily identify their position in the process of meeting the needs of visitors grouped according to strategic visitor flows. Moreover, the ability to access the virtual presence of stakeholders makes it easier to realise if all the services that visitors use and attractions they visit are part of the destination. This may result in changes in the boundaries of a destination.

The graphical representation on the digital map also provides a better overview of the situation in a destination and justifies the need to involve stakeholders in meeting the needs of the identified visitor flows. Being able to find and analyse a rich portfolio of visitor flows and the network of the most important stakeholders that are able to attract these flows can lead to more adaptive and resilient tourism systems. In this way, the smart approach based on data analytics brings more knowledge to flow-based destination management and helps to build a more resilient destination. Moreover, it allows incorporating the actual dynamics of tourist flows, which are the origins of destination development and the basis for destination design.

References

Asero, V., Gozzo, S., and Tomaselli, V., 2016. Building tourism networks through tourist mobility. *Journal of Travel Research*, 55 (6), 751–763.

Baggio, R., 2013. Studying complex tourism systems: a novel approach based on networks derived from a time series. *In: International Academic Conference on Economic and Social Development*. Moscow.

Baggio, R., 2017. Network science and tourism – The state of the art. *Tourism Review*, 72 (1), 120–131.

Baggio, R., and Sainaghi, R., 2016. Mapping time series into networks as a tool to assess the complex dynamics of tourism systems. *Tourism Management*, 54, 23–33.

Baggio, R., and Scaglione, M., 2018. Strategic visitor flows and destination management organization. *Information Technology and Tourism*, 18 (1–4), 29–42.

Beritelli, P., 2019. Transferring concepts and tools from other fields to the tourist destination: A critical viewpoint focusing on the lifecycle concept. *Journal of Destination Marketing and Management*, 14 (2019), 100384.

Beritelli, P., Crescini, G., Reinhold, S., and Schanderl, V., 2019. *How flow-based destination management blends theory and method for practical impact*. Cham: Springer, 289–310.

Beritelli, P., and Laesser, C., 2017. The dynamics of destinations and tourism development. *In*: D.R. Fesenmaier, and Z. Xiang, eds. *Design science in tourism, tourism on the verge*. Cham: Springer International Publishing Switzerland, 195–214.

Beritelli, P., Laesser, C., Reinhold, S., and Kappler, A., 2013. *Das St. Galler modell fur destinationsmanagement: Geschäftsmodellinnovation in netzwerken*. St. Gallen: IMP-HSF.

Beritelli, P., Reinhold, S., and Laesser, C., 2020. Visitor flows, trajectories and corridors: Planning and designing places from the traveler's point of view. *Annals of Tourism Research*, 82 (April), 102936.

Borgatti, S., Everett, M., and Johnson, J., 2018. *Analysing social networks*. 2nd edition. London: SAGE Publications.

Cvelbar, L.K., Mayr, M., and Vavpotic, D., 2018. Geographical mapping of visitor flow in tourism: A user-generated content approach. *Tourism Economics*, 24 (6), 701–719.

Duan, W., Mu, W., and Bu, H., 2017. "Big data" versus "small data" in social sciences. *Chinese Sociological Dialogue*, 2 (3–4), 98–119.

Gonçalves, B.A., Carpi, L., Rosso, O.A., and Ravetti, M.G., 2016. Time series characterization via horizontal visibility graph and Information Theory. *Physica A: Statistical Mechanics and its Applications*, 464, 93–102.

Hwang, Y.H., Gretzel, U., and Fesenmaier, D.R., 2006. Multicity trip patterns. Tourists to the United States. *Annals of Tourism Research*, 33 (4), 1057–1078.

Kitchin, R., and Lauriault, T.P., 2015. Small data in the era of big data. *Geo Journal*, 80 (4), 463–475.

Koens, K., Smit, B., and Melissen, F., 2021. Designing destinations for good: Using design roadmapping to support pro-active destination development. *Annals of Tourism Research*, 89, 103233.

116   *The contribution of smart approach*

Li, Z., Lee, J.G., Li, X., and Han, J., 2010. Incremental clustering for trajectories. *In*: Kitagawa H., Ishikawa Y., Li Q., Watanabe C., eds. *Lecture notes in computer science*. Berlin, Heidelberg: Springer, 32–46.

Newman, M.E.J., 2003. Mixing patterns in networks. *Physical Review E - Statistical Physics, Plasmas, Fluids, and Related Interdisciplinary Topics*, 67 (2), 13.

Oussous, A., Benjelloun, F.Z., Ait Lahcen, A., and Belfkih, S., 2018. Big Data technologies: A survey. *Journal of King Saud University - Computer and Information Sciences*, 30 (4), 431–448.

Park, S., Xu, Y., Jiang, L., Chen, Z., and Huang, S., 2020. Spatial structures of tourism destinations: A trajectory data mining approach leveraging mobile big data. *Annals of Tourism Research*, 84 (September 2020), 102973.

Park, S., and Zhong, R.R., 2021. Pattern recognition of travel mobility in a city destination: Application of network motif analytics. *Journal of Travel Research*.

Reinhold, S., Beritelli, P., and Grünig, R., 2019. A business model typology for destination management organizations. *Tourism Review*, 74 (6), 1135–1152.

Ricciato, F., Wirthmann, A., and Hahn, M., 2020. Trusted smart statistics: How new data will change official statistics. *Data & Policy*, 2 (May 2021).

Shih, H.Y., 2006. Network characteristics of drive tourism destinations: An application of network analysis in tourism. *Tourism Management*, 27 (5), 1029–1039.

Part 3

Designing smart tourism destination governance towards sustainability, competitiveness and resilience

Governing a destination towards sustainability, competitiveness and resilience is essentially more and more a matter of designing and implementing structures and processes considering diverse systemic challenges. Tourism destinations do not originate on the marketer's desk, but they are the result of creative design and development schemes (Gunn 1972). Destination design strengthens the importance of gathering demand and supply data to assist decision-making. Data should be used to develop knowledge to aid planning and development (O'Leary & Fesenmaier 2017). In this way, the design approach enables the detection, description and support of creative and non-linear tourism planning based on the study of tourists and stakeholders both in their spatial and relational context (Scuttari et al. 2021), thus better steering the destination development.

Empirical analysis of the contribution of the smart approach to overcoming the challenges of destination governance revealed several important issues. The relatively simple understanding of a changing tourist behaviour can be changed by the possibilities of data collection along the tourist journey in real time. Thanks to technology acceptance and use by the majority of tourist segments, DMOs and destination stakeholders have enough data to co-create a personalised experience and react to changing tourist behaviour. Moreover, the technology savvy tourists behave in a more sustainable way. The development of ICTs and the more complex requirements of tourists and stakeholders challenge the main role of DMOs. The smart tourism ecosystem, in which DMOs operate, stimulates the role of knowledge transfer. DMOs have the ability to become leaders in knowledge transfer and together with inter-stakeholder collaboration; these roles are becoming vital for DMOs. This leads to higher competitiveness of a

DOI: 10.4324/9781003269342-9

destination. Moreover, attention to the supply side of the destination and defined destination boundaries create several problems that tourism destination governance has to face. Thanks to technologies used for data collection and analysis, the identification of strategic visitor flows and the ability to find the intersection between destination demand and supply is easier. This creates new possibilities of enriching flow-based destination management and results in greater resilience of a destination. This contribution of smart approach provides opportunities for designing new perspectives for smart destination governance.

The third part of the book proposes the design-based perspectives for smart tourism destination governance. It highlights that destination governance should take into account the dynamic environment in which the destination is embedded, problems of cooperation and networking in a destination, the growing importance of visitor flows and the influence of the remarkable advances and availability of technological tools (Baggio 2020). The transformation of tourists from passive recipients towards active co-creators of experiences needs to be considered in smart destination governance. So far, the information on tourists in many destinations has been limited, not allowing to co-create the experience in real time. Moreover, the application of information technologies for better collaboration can be a way to overcome top-down coordination and redistribute the decision-making among destination stakeholders. In order to achieve better governance, smart solutions in the processing of information and decision-making could be applied to design tourist experiences and strengthen the collaborative design, thus applying new perspectives for smart destination governance.

References

Baggio, R., 2020. Tourism destinations: A universality conjecture based on network science. *Annals of Tourism Research*, 82 (April), 102929.

Gunn, C., 1972. *Vacationscape: Designing tourist areas.* Austin: Bureau of Business Research, University of Texas at Austin.

O'Leary, J.T., and Fesenmaier, D., 2017. Concluding remarks: Tourism design and the future of tourism. *In*: D. Fesenmaier, and Z. Xiang, eds. *Design science in tourism.* Cham: Springer, 265–272.

Scuttari, A., Pechlaner, H., and Erschbamer, G., 2021. Destination design: A heuristic case study approach to sustainability-oriented innovation. *Annals of Tourism Research*, 86 (June 2020), 103068.

6   Designing tourist experience based on smart data

One of the greatest difficulties in analysing tourist behaviour has been limited access to complete information, rather a collection of fragments has been combined to produce valuable information (Cousin et al. 2017). So far, destination managers have relied mainly on accommodation statistics and knowingly and intentionally provided explicit tourist feedback based on field surveys and e-reviews (Fuchs et al. 2014). This relatively simple understanding of tourist behaviour, focusing also mainly on dreaming, searching and post-trip experiences, resulted mainly in creating standardised products and marketing communication. However, the design approach stresses that the overriding principle of tourism development must be more sensitive to the feelings and attitudes of tourists as entire persons (Gunn 1972). The advantage of the smart approach is the examination of the 'black box' – the soul of the tourists and the process of decision-making, which leads to greater transparency of the process comparing the traditional examination of tourist models (Gajdošík et al. 2021).

The analysis of touchpoints along the tourist journey and the segmentation of tourists based on information technology use and acceptance revealed that the majority of tourists are keen to use technologies during the trip. This creates opportunities to collect real-time information about tourist behaviour in all travel phases, enabling co-creation, personalised experience and targeted communication. Moreover, with the continual rise of smart technologies, the tourist is no longer isolated in a limited zone of knowledge while travelling (Fan et al. 2019). Dynamic big data mining and artificial intelligence, together with emotional intelligence, can identify in real time what each tourist wants (Buhalis & Sinarta 2019), leading to a better understanding of a tourist behaviour, which can lead to instant data-driven consumer-centric value and experience co-creation (Assiouras et al. 2019; Zhang et al. 2018). It leads to more possibilities to better use of all destination

DOI: 10.4324/9781003269342-10

resources to offer a more human, richer and more meaningful experience, as a basic principle of destination design (Gunn 1972). Moreover, information technologies can positively influence tourists towards sustainable behaviour.

6.1 Co-creating experience during all trip experience phases

Based on empirical analysis, it can be stated that the majority of tourists are accustomed to using information technologies during all the trip experience phases. The willingness to co-create and share data leads to the need of personalised solutions, while reviews, authentic experiences and UGC are becoming crucial in the destination selection process. In this context, experience makes a useful conceptualisation to access the competitiveness and economic success of a destination (Shoval & Birenboim 2019).

Many DMOs and destination stakeholders in Europe and North America consider the planning and booking stage of the trip experience phases as a top priority for their digital strategies (Trekksoft 2017). While organisations should not ignore this phase, they have to acknowledge that they simply cannot compete with the giants, who have much larger budgets (e.g. Google, Booking.com, Expedia) and established brands. From a digital point of view, for tourists, each phase is important and should be addressed. Therefore, the business models of DMOs should be changed towards creating value propositions during all trip experience phases based on personalisation and experience enrichment.

In the planning and booking phase, the competition is the toughest. IDS/OTAs have a very strong position on the market, leaving DMOs and individual stakeholders behind. However, in order to reach the global market, these organisations use standardised products and due to their presence only in the first phase (planning and booking), they are not able to collect digital footprints along the whole tourist journey. Therefore, there is an opportunity for DMO and other destination stakeholders to take advantage of their presence along the whole tourist journey. Destination websites should be transformed into smart web portals. These portals should be able to filter suitable information and learn from processes to provide users with explicit and customised information and services (Zhang et al. 2018). It can be done by using artificial intelligence (AI) tools, such as anticipatory product customisation, collaborative filtering or text analysis. With the help of AI, digital footprints of each tourist can be used to understand needs, budget and travel preferences in order to suggest the right product and provide the tourist with relevant information to facilitate the decision-making in a complex environment. Based on the available data on tourists, DMO or other stakeholders can pre-create and display the tailor-made product to each tourist or use that kind of language that visitor consumes to affect a personalised experience. The portal should be connected to the major review sites, allowing the user to browse the customer reviews. The use of user-generated visuals to attract and engage tourists is welcomed, while the application of AI and machine learning to UGC can ensure that only relevant photos and videos are displayed. Moreover, the changing content of the portal can promote personalised sustainable alternatives for each tourist.

The staying phase should be built on authentic experience, which can range from ecological, adventurous or local experience to unique experience. The experience in destinations should be developed from staging experience and passive experience consumption, to co-creation or even the self-direction of experience, where DMOs provide only the tools for the active self-experience production of the tourist (Gelter 2017). It can be done by creating destination apps incorporating the most common requirements of the majority of tourists and the state-of-the-art technologies, such as digital map, real-time position monitoring, listings of attractions and tourism businesses in a destination, augmented reality and social media integration. With geolocation information, mobile apps can offer users timely information, offers and promotions (Qin et al. 2017). Providing the app with artificial intelligence enables understanding tourist habits and preferences in order to offer personalised experiences. Moreover, mobile apps and smart portals can steer the tourist behaviour by providing tourists with suitable information (e.g. promoting less visited places in the peak times or redirecting travel routes based on congestions in a destination). Using mobile apps for gamification in a destination allows to deeply connect the tourist with experiencing a destination. Using location-based services allows to access location-specific information to easily discover a destination and provide interesting contextual information (historical facts, stories). This experience can be enriched by the support of wearables, where a well-informed tourist with extended cognitive abilities can become a smart explorer. The use of wearables will influence destination governance in terms of programming, guiding and information provision to tourists and enables the space-time relevant recommendation systems (Tussyadiah 2014).

Traditionally, the post-travelling phase has been left to a tourist with his photos, videos and souvenirs physically shared among friends.

With the massive use of social media, sharing the experience in forms of status updates, comments, photos and videos, is gaining importance and significantly affects the reputation of a destination. In order to govern a destination in a smart way, online reputation management should be embraced. It involves interacting with tourists online, creating shareable content, monitoring what tourists are saying, keeping track of their dialogue, addressing negative content found online and following up on ideas that are shared through social media (Dijkmans et al. 2015). However, the volume of UGC on social media reached a level that makes manual processing almost impossible, creating a demand for new analytical approaches, such as sentiment analysis applied to text and visuals. Artificial intelligence tools can highlight frequently used words, distinguish sentiment, as well as look at the correlation of certain words. Artificial intelligence-based platforms (e.g. Metis) can help to dig into tourist feedback, measure performance and instantly discover what really matters to tourists. Real-time analysis of tourist feedback can detect underlying problems and lead to more sustainable development.

6.2 Reacting to tourist behaviour in real time

Based on information on tourists and their behaviour, their experience can be co-created. For tourists, technology represents an opportunity to actively participate in destination activities and to take part in the construction of its own experience. However, the great challenges designers and decision-makers have to face is to lead tourists into a strong and subtle environment and to provide them with experiences that are meaningful, pleasurable and fruitful (Gunn 1997). Therefore, the experience design should be based on a real-time reaction to changes in tourist behaviour.

As reviews on social media are the most important decisive factor when choosing a destination, the content on social media can be a supplement tool to passive mobile positioning analysing the changes in tourist behaviour in real time. Data from social media can be extracted using APIs. Examining the presence of an API is critical, as it eases the data collection and integration process. The API documentation provides information on data that are accessible through different API endpoints (Owuor & Hochmair 2020) (Table 6.1).

In order to analyse the mobility of visitor flows, three types of data are needed. Firstly, it is the user identifier (ID), then the date and time of creating the examined content (time stamp) and finally the data concerning the geolocation (latitude and longitude). In order to

Table 6.1 The most used APIs to collect information on social media

Social Media	API(s)	Limit	Location data
Facebook	Graph	varies	place name, coordinates
Flickr	Flickr rest	3,600 queries/ hour	coordinates
Instagram	Basic display, Graph	varies	coordinates
Pinterest	Pinterest	160 calls/day	place name
Twitter	Search tweets	varies	place name, coordinates

analyse the data, destination boundaries need to be set using the 'Bounding Box' command. It is a comma-separated list of four values that define the bounding box of the geographic area of destination that will be searched when the metadata is downloaded. The four values represent the lower-left corner of the field – minimum longitude (minimum_longitude), minimum latitude (minimum_latitude) and the upper right corner – maximum longitude (maximum_longitude), maximum latitude (maximum_latitude) (Figure 6.1).

The geographic space defined in this way will be searched and the data of all photos created in that space will be downloaded. Subsequently, the individual photos are loaded, along with their data,

```
# connecting to Flickr
flickr = FlickrAPI(key, secret, format='parsed-json')

i = 1
while True:
    result = flickr.photos.search(
        #text = 'your keyword',      #keyword change
        per_page = 400,              #number of data per page
        has_geo = 1,                 #Photo that has geo location
        min_taken_date = min_taken_date,
        max_taken_date = max_taken_date,
        #woe id = 7153351, #7153351 # woeid does not work.
        bbox = '-122.42307100000001,37.773779,-122.381071,37.815779',
        media = 'photos',            # collecting photos without video
        sort = 'date-taken-desc',        # collecting photos from latest
        privacy_filter =1,
        safe_search = 1,             # photos without violence
        extras = 'geo,url_n,date_taken,views, license',
        page = i
    )
```

Figure 6.1 Specifying the destination boundaries for social media analytics by Bounding Box.

such as the ID and geographical coordinates, which create a dataset suitable for further research.

Besides APIs, there are several tools for social media analytics available for non-technicians. These tools provide online dashboards or downloadable datasets for destination managers and include indicators such as the number of mentions, source, location, sentiment, reach or influence score, which help to better understand tourist behaviour. Moreover, data can be exported to the database for further analysis. Among the most used tools belong MediaToolkit, Hootsuite and Keyhole.

To illustrate the importance of social media monitoring, the social media analytics using the business analytics tool (MediaToolkit) in The High Tatras is used as an example (Figure 6.2).

Time series of influence score, based on comments using official hashtags #High Tatras and #Vysoke Tatry from Facebook, Instagram, Twitter, Web and TripAdvisor were exported using business analytics tools. Together, 161 posts from 25 October to 24 November 2020 were collected. As the destination and its dynamics are seen as complex systems and concerning the proved applicability of mapping time series into networks, the non-linear approach was used to transform time series into a network. Further analysis revealed five communities (Figure 6.3). Based on these communities, turning points in time series were identified showing when the influence of the posts started to change. These changes can be subsequently paired with the situation in a destination, showing which factors influenced these changes (e.g. viral photos).

Moreover, if a tourist expresses frustration on social media, the AI tool can analyse the tourist intent and context to automatically reach out with real-time interventions that are most likely to deliver a positive impact. These interventions can range from providing additional information, helping the tourist to understand the situation, to suggesting more options that can meet the requirement of the tourist.

The data from social media can be analysed by AI and further steps can be taken to steer the tourist behaviour. Photos uploaded by tourists can be used to detect the attendance of tourist attractions or to estimate environmental impacts. Based on these data, tourists can get personalised recommendations on which attraction is worth visiting and where not to go. The AI helps to identify different objects in photos of tourists (e.g. people, pollution) and compare them with the photo database of the destination. Based on this comparison, appropriate reactions can be made in order to ensure sustainable development (Figure 6.4).

	TIME	DATE	SOURCE_TYPE	FROM	AUTHOR	TITLE	LANGUAGES	LOCATIONS	AUTO_SENTIMENT	REACH	INFLUENCE_SCORE
2	06:26:00	2020-11-24	web	sme.sk	Petit Press a.s.	Slovaks: Getting t	en	SK	positive	8188	8
3	18:27:00	2020-11-23	facebook	Región Vysoké Tatry - High T	Región Vysoké Tatry - High T	Pograd - oficiálna	sk	SK	positive	771	4
4	09:06:15	2020-11-23	facebook	Región Vysoké Tatry - High T	Región Vysoké Tatry - High T	Lyžiarske stredisk.sk		SK	neutral	771	4
5	03:36:22	2020-11-22	instagram	anonymous_user	anonymous_user	Do you like nature	en, sk	SK, US	positive	90	1
6	14:00:58	2020-11-20	web	fargomonthly.com	@fargomonthly	Think Global, Act	en	US	positive	2	1
7	12:15:59	2020-11-20	web	creotour.sk		svet cestovania	sk	SK	positive	1	1
8	12:02:00	2020-11-20	web	sme.sk	Petit Press a.s.	Roundup: The wo	en	SK	positive	2456	8
9	08:29:40	2020-11-20	facebook	Región Vysoké Tatry - High T	Región Vysoké Tatry - High T	Od dnešného dňa	sk	SK	positive	747	4
10	23:35:03	2020-11-19	twitter	Amazing Slovakia	Amazing Slovakia	Thanks to pilot M	en, und	SK	positive	92	1
11	21:45:26	2020-11-19	twitter	Kimber	Kimber	RT @slovakspect	en, und	CZ	positive	60	1
12	12:44:29	2020-11-19	web	waszaturystyka.pl	https://www.faceboc	Dzisiaj otwarcie Ś	pl	PL	positive	2	1
13	12:34:31	2020-11-19	twitter	Slovenčina pro Čechy	Slovenčina pro Čechy	To, jak dnes vypar	cs	CZ	positive	40	1
14	02:41:00	2020-11-19	web	docplayer.pl		VI ZIMOWY MARÚ	pl	PL	neutral	123	4
15	00:54:43	2020-11-19	web	tin247.com		5 hiện tượng thiêr	vietnamese, vi	VN		84	4
16	00:52:33	2020-11-19	web	doanhnghiepvn.vn		5 hiện tượng thiêr	vi	VN		0	1
17	21:02:54	2020-11-18	twitter	Viktor Neginskiy	Theo Vy Vy/VietQ	Thanks to pilot M	en, und	US	positive	35	1
18	21:01:06	2020-11-18	twitter	The Slovak Spectator	Viktor Neginskiy	Thanks to pilot M	en, und	SK	positive	267	2
19	21:01:03	2020-11-18	facebook	The Slovak Spectator	The Slovak Spectator	Spectacular Slova	en	US	positive	438	3
20	11:52:00	2020-11-18	web	sme.sk	Petit Press a.s.	Tatra peaks and v	en	SK	positive	9825	8
21	20:46:10	2020-11-17	web	medium.com	https://talkingforests.	Treetop Walkway	en	US	negative	13	10
22	19:02:28	2020-11-17	youtube	Marian Sikky Chmel	Marian Sikky Chmel	Hike'n' Flair	Flai	en	US	positive	96	1
23	17:00:11	2020-11-17	youtube	DEEJAY MILO	DEEJAY MILO	TUBLATANKA - Ni	sk	SK	positive	0	1
24	05:40:54	2020-11-17	twitter	The Tour Team	The Tour Team	Happy Monday! Š	en, und	US	positive	4	1

Figure 6.2 Example of dataset used for social media analytics using Mediatoolkit.

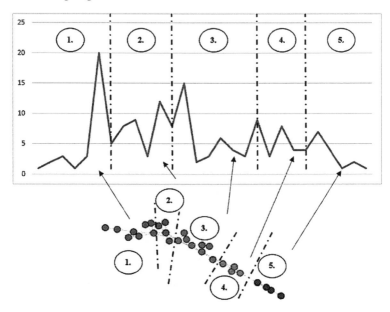

Figure 6.3 Identification of turning points in time series using modularity
analysis of the network.

The real-time data can be obtained also from mobile apps. Integration of social media features and location sharing functions can
bring additional information on tourist behaviour. Travel patterns can
be accessed by the analysis of movement based on location-based services (e.g. GPS). Even if a destination does not have its own mobile
app, it is possible to use some third-party apps using GPX files. A
GPX file (GPS Exchange Format) is a specific XML file designed as a
GPS data format for software applications. It is used to describe routes
and waypoints. It contains geographical coordinates and can also
include data on altitude, time, speed of movement, colour of tourist
signs, place description, landmarks, etc. Such a file can be opened in
GPS devices, in a smartphone or wearables. It is mainly used for sports
activities such as cross-country skiing, hiking and cycling; therefore, it
is applicable in recreational destinations. Analysis of the number of
downloads of GPX files can be an additional source of information
about the visitor flows.

Moreover, data from destination cards, bank cards or traffic cards
can bring valuable information to urban destinations. Each validation
of the card contains card ID, date and used services. Apart from basic

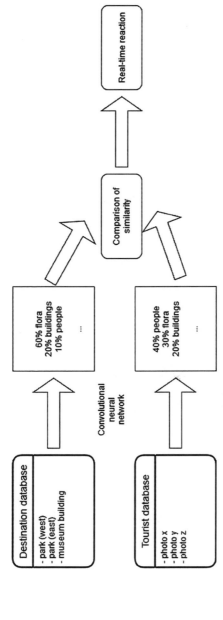

Figure 6.4 Real-time reaction based on AI used on visuals.

analytics such as the number of issued cards and the number of guests, several data mining approaches can be used to analyse the behaviour of tourists. These techniques should extract transactions in log files. Time thresholds can be adopted to link these transactions and to create and separate different trips. As boundary data, the defined maximum times for the different trips can be used with the 95th percentile transaction time difference. Moreover, the Hierarchical Ascending clustering method can be used to create a group of tourists with similar geospatial behaviour (e.g. visited attractions) and travel characteristics (e.g. frequency of card use).

6.3 Using smart data for value co-creation

Following these approaches, destination managers have enough data to react to changing tourist behaviour. They have the opportunity to recognise the need to estimate the value of their data and manage data accordingly to their value. Therefore, there is a challenge to shift attention from 'big' to 'smart' data, adding layers of information, facilitating real-time usage and appropriate dissemination of trends (Volo 2020). Smart data is a subset of data (big or small) valuable for an organisation. The purpose of smart data is to hold the valuable data and use them to interact in real time (Iafrate 2014). Smart data should be seen as the set of methodologies and techniques that enable extracting all the value from the data (Sheth 2014). While big data focuses mainly on the management of volume, velocity and variety of data, smart data focuses on the veracity and value dimensions. Smart data filters out the noise and retain only the data valuable to solve problems, which gives personalised and actionable information (Baldassarre et al. 2018).

Based on smart data, managers can analyse changes in tourist behaviour, find out which and what kind of posts influence the most, what are the most visited attractions and thus make appropriate changes in designing tourist experience. Real-time analytics allows timely reaction, which is not possible with traditional techniques of data collection. Traditional techniques, which are based on static and ad hoc data (accommodation statistics, questionnaire surveys) do not provide sufficient information for the right decisions. Moreover, these data are available retrospectively, which does not allow making timely decisions. Dynamic data and real-time analytics allow to be more proactive, rather reactive.

From the tourist perspective, the personalised information strengthens the experience, while from the governance perspective, the

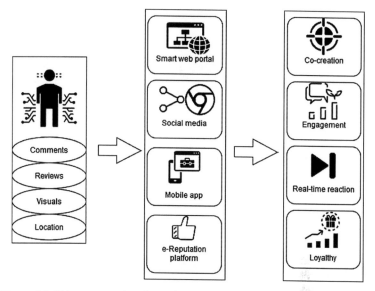

Figure 6.5 Value co-creation through smart data in a destination.

real-time data enables to steer and manage the visitor behaviour. With the massive use of information technologies through the trip experience phases, organisations have real-time information on searches, bookings, movements and sentiments of tourists, which create opportunities for value co-creation (Figure 6.5).

Touchpoints along the tourist journey need to be carefully designed to enhance the co-creation of value between stakeholders and tourists. Co-creating personalised experiences increase the demand for the product and thus create revenue opportunities. Integrating booking engines into smart portals and mobile apps provides additional income, which can be used for destination development, while intermediaries (IDS/OTA) use it for their own purposes. Smart portals, apps and the support of augmented reality give organisations in a destination, full control of the tourist experience and thus create engagement. Together with online reputation management, it strengthens the loyalty of tourists.

To summarise, designing a tourist experience based on data supports the smart approach to destination governance. In order to compete with global players on the online market, DMOs and destination stakeholders should co-create a personalised experience with tourists during all the trip experience phases. Moreover, it is important to make decisions using smart data on tourists, which positively influence the value co-creation in a destination. This new perspective on smart data enables a faster and more accurate reaction of managers to demand changes in a destination. Destination governance is entering the new age of innovation and value co-creation through information technologies and data analytics, where big data analytics and the application of AI tools are welcomed.

References

Assiouras, I., Skourtis, G., Giannopoulos, A., Buhalis, D., and Koniordos, M., 2019. Value co-creation and customer citizenship behavior. *Annals of Tourism Research*, 78 (September 2019), 102742.

Baldassarre, M.T., Garcia, B.R., Caballero, I., Caivano, D., and Piattini, M., 2018. From big data to smart data: A data quality perspective. *In*: A. Bucchiarone, M. Mongiello, and F. Nocera, eds. *EnSEmble 2018 - Proceedings of the 1st ACM SIGSOFT International workshop on ensemble-based software engineering, co-located with FSE 2018*. Lake Buena Vista FL USA: Association for Computing Machinery, 19–24.

Buhalis, D., and Sinarta, Y., 2019. Real-time co-creation and nowness service: Lessons from tourism and hospitality. *Journal of Travel & Tourism Marketing*, 36 (5), 563–582.

Cousin, S., Chareyron, G., and Jacquot, S., 2017. Big data and tourism. *In*: L. Lowry, ed. *The SAGE international encyclopedia of travel and tourism*. Thousand Oaks: SAGE Publications, 151–155.

Dijkmans, C., Kerkhof, P., and Beukeboom, C.J., 2015. A stage to engage: Social media use and corporate reputation. *Tourism Management*, 47, 58–67.

Fan, D.X.F., Buhalis, D., and Lin, B., 2019. A tourist typology of online and face-to-face social contact: Destination immersion and tourism encapsulation/decapsulation. *Annals of Tourism Research*, 78, 102757.

Fuchs, M., Höpken, W., and Lexhagen, M., 2014. Big data analytics for knowledge generation in tourism destinations – A case from Sweden. *Journal of Destination Marketing & Management*, 3 (4), 198–209.

Gajdošík, T., Maráková, V., and Kučerová, J., 2021. From mass tourists to smart tourists: A perspective article. *Tourism Review*, 76 (1), 47–50.

Gelter, H., 2017. *Digital tourism - An analysis of digital trends in tourism and customer digital mobile behaviour* Oslo: Visit Artic Europe.

Gunn, C., 1972. *Vacationscape: Designing tourist areas*. Austin: Bureau of Business Research, University of Texas at Austin.

Gunn, C., 1997. *Vacationscape: Developing tourist areas*. 3rd edition. Washington: Routledge.

Iafrate, F., 2014. A journey from big data to smart data. *In*: P.J. Benghozi, D. Krob, A. Lonjon, and H. Panetto, eds. *Advances in intelligent systems and computing*. Cham: Springer International Publishing, 25–33.

Owuor, I., and Hochmair, H.H., 2020. An overview of social media apps and their potential role in geospatial research. *ISPRS International Journal of Geo-Information*, 9 (9), 526.

Qin, M., Tang, C.H., Jang, S., and Lehto, X., 2017. Mobile app introduction and shareholder returns. *Journal of Hospitality and Tourism Management*, 31, 173–180.

Sheth, A., 2014. Transforming big data into smart data: Deriving value via harnessing volume, variety, and velocity using semantic techniques and technologies. *In: 2014 IEEE 30th International Conference on Data Engineering*. Chicago, IL, USA: Institute of Electrical and Electronics Engineers (IEEE), 2–2.

Shoval, N., and Birenboim, A., 2019. Customization and augmentation of experiences through mobile technologies. *Tourism Economics*, 25 (5), 661–669.

Trekksoft, 2017. *Making experiences the cornerstone of destination marketing* Barcelona: Trekksoft.

Tussyadiah, I., 2014. Expectation of travel experiences with wearable computing devices. *In: Z. Xiang, and I. Tussyadiah, eds. Information and communication technologies in tourism 2014*. Cham: Springer International Publishing Switzerland, 539–552.

Volo, S., 2020. Tourism statistics, indicators and big data: A perspective article. *Tourism Review*, 75 (1), 304–309.

Zhang, H., Gordon, S., Buhalis, D., and Ding, X., 2018. Experience value cocreation on destination online platforms. *Journal of Travel Research*, 57 (8), 1093–1107.

Zhang, T., Cheung, C., and Law, R., 2018. Functionality evaluation for destination marketing websites in smart tourism cities. *Journal of China Tourism Research*, 14 (3), 263–278.

7 Strengthening collaborative design through smart solutions

Apart from designing unique tourist experiences, it is essential to use the smart approach in order to design solutions that satisfy destination stakeholders. The collaborative design with the help of information technology can be a useful tool for strengthening the smart destination governance. Information sharing and cooperation are the main elements in framing the use of technologies to enable collaborative governance (Pereira et al. 2018). Therefore, collaborative design should be reflected in the creation of networks for dialogue among stakeholders in a destination through the use of technology, which is proposed as an important strategy for governance (Cizel et al. 2016). Applying such smart principles in a destination can create a knowledge-based destination, where knowledge transfer is an important element of destination competitiveness (Baggio & Cooper 2010).

Recognising visitor flows in destinations enables to construct collaborative design associating those stakeholders and touchpoints tourists are likely to visit in their trajectory. This kind of design would help destination managers to reduce costs and tourists to enhance their experience (Park et al. 2020). In this sense, service blueprinting can be used to add value to cooperation between stakeholders by identifying stakeholders and their roles in attracting specified visitor flows.

To proceed with the vast amount of data collected and to strengthen the knowledge transfer in a destination, there is a need for a technological platform on which information related to tourism activities could be collected and exchanged instantly and which will dynamically interconnect destination stakeholders (Buhalis & Amaranggana 2015). This kind of information system should be able to obtain information from physical and digital sources and, with the combination of advanced technologies, be capable of transforming the data into experiences and business value propositions focused on efficiency, sustainability and experience enrichment (Gretzel et al. 2015). It should also

DOI: 10.4324/9781003269342-11

facilitate the touchpoints with the tourists by allowing the connection through a wide range of end-user devices supporting tourist experiences (Buonincontri & Micera 2016).

7.1 Augmented service blueprinting in a destination

The role of all destination stakeholders is important for the success of a destination. Following the results of the analysis of the dynamic construct of a destination, the DMO should help the destination stakeholders to find their position in attracting identified visitor flows. Moreover, from an ecosystem perspective, it is important to identify the relationships between stakeholders, which can lead to improvement in service efficacy and effectiveness. The ecosystem actors and their engagement touchpoints need to be conceptualised and contribute to stakeholder selection (Eichelberger et al. 2020). In this sense, service blueprinting is a useful tool, emphasising the value of coordination and cooperation among destination stakeholders that are able to attract visitor flows (Beritelli et al. 2013).

Service blueprinting is a design-oriented method used to analyse the detailed process of service delivery from the supplier point of view. This model is able to visually depict objectives and steps in the service delivery process, set out individual service responsibilities and examine possible failures in the process, thus improving the service design. Based on the analysis of touchpoints along tourist journey, the blueprint should consider service delivery through both offline and online touchpoints. So far, the method of blueprinting has been used mainly from the business perspective; however, it has great potential in collaborative destination design.

Taking a supplier's viewpoint on the dynamic construct of a destination, destination stakeholders should first understand what tourists do, where they stay and why they are in a particular place (Beritelli 2019). With the help of information technology, they are able to easily find strategic visitor flows and understand their behaviour and movement. On the basis of the identification of flows, strategic business areas can be defined.

Visited attractions and activities performed at a destination act as business areas. Each business area is characterised by a specific visitor flow, which shares similar motivations and activities. Those business areas that can be located, that are time-limited and strategically important for a destination are called strategic business areas. In the background of strategic business areas, there is a system of private and public stakeholders that work together to create value for the visitor

(Beritelli et al. 2013). From the destination governance perspective, the support must start with identifying strategic business areas in a destination, which is a precondition to designing and setting the stage for different performances (experience design and service design) (Beritelli et al. 2020) (Table 7.1).

Thanks to the smart approach, the identification of strategic business areas is easier and less time-consuming. Social media and web analytics can be used to deeply analyse the profiles of visitors. Passive mobile positioning, destination apps, or smart cards are useful sources of data for the identification of source markets, time, length of tourist stay and area visited. Based on these data sources, different visitor flows in a destination can be constructed and subsequently, strategic business areas can be identified.

In addition, for each strategic business area, it is necessary to define which stakeholders can attract the specified visitor flow and what their managerial and marketing tasks are. The digital map of a destination and the destination management system are useful data sources for this analysis. The advantage of this analysis is that it makes it easier to identify areas of interest and focus from the perspective of stakeholders. This will allow better coordination of projects and speed up cooperation among actors.

In order to clarify the tasks and identify priorities in steering visitor flows and co-creating tourist experiences, the augmented service blueprint in a destination should be created. The augmentation in service blueprinting focuses on the interaction between tourists and different physical (offline) and digital (online) touchpoints as a result of high technology use and acceptance by tourists, as well as it takes into account the use of virtual environments (Table 7.2).

During each stage of a tourist journey, the expected tourist experience and service provision should be identified. Services offered by destination stakeholders constitute the building blocks for experience creation in a destination. This kind of performance allows the identification of offline and online touchpoints and further assigns the responsibility of each stakeholder in a destination. Stakeholders are able to easily identify their position in service provision for tourists and find out which other services in a destination are used by tourists. Service blueprinting on a destination level allows to realise that stakeholders themselves cannot satisfy the requirements of a specified tourist flow and that cooperation is needed.

However, cooperation in a destination has several barriers. To overcome the barriers of cooperation among stakeholders, a design-based serious gaming approach can be introduced. This approach combines

Table 7.1 Example of strategic business areas identification based on visitor flows

Criteria	SBA- Winter Sports	SBA – MICE	Data Collection and Analysis
Visitor profile	Young and active tourist	Business travellers	Social media and web analytics
Source market	Domestic tourists, tourists from neighbouring countries	Tourists from neighbouring countries	Mobile positioning (roaming), destination app, smart card
Time	Winter season	Off season	social media analytics, mobile positioning, destination app, smart card
Length of stay	2–4 nights	5–6 nights	Mobile positioning, destination app, smart card
Area visited			Mobile positioning (DBSCAN), destination app, smart card, network analysis
Stakeholders			Online geographic information system and destination management system

Table 7.2 Service blueprint in a destination

Phase	Experience	Service	Offline Touchpoints	Online Touchpoints	Responsibility
Planning and booking	Feel excited and inspired with personalised advice	Provide tourists suitable information and find inspiration	TV, radio, newspapers, word of mouth	Social media, websites,	DMO, accommodation facilities, cultural facilities
	Save time and money while booking	Ensure booking assistance	Travel agencies	IDS/OTA, booking engine on websites,	DMO, accommodation facilities
	Feel welcome and oriented	Ensure a welcoming experience and personalised information	Tourist information office, residents	Websites, mobile apps with digital maps, social media	DMO, tourist information office, residents
Staying in a destination	Feel confident	Help to find and book authentic and memorable activities	Tourist information office	Destination management system	DMO, tourist information office,
	Get on-demand assistance	Provide quality service	Employees of service providers	Website	Accommodation, catering, sport and recreational facilities
Sharing experiences	Feel good about the visit Share memories	Provide possibilities for feedback	Mail, telephone survey	Social media, newsletter	Accommodation facilities, DMO

the principles of play and gaming to achieve objectives with the ability to learn and cooperate in a safe environment of a simplified representation of reality.

This kind of game can be a mixture of a physical playing field (game board, 3D-printed miniatures of destination attractions) and a virtual field (virtual reality, digital simulation model). The gaming activities comprise adjustments in the destination infrastructure (building, renovating, removing) and policy-based actions (e.g. regulations, visitor flow management). Stakeholders have the possibility to communicate, discuss and try to govern a destination based on the game activities thanks to the physical board game. The virtual environment can stimulate a deep connection with the real world and simulate the effects of proposed decisions. This innovative method is able to stimulate open and direct communication among stakeholders by creating a specific experience where different stakeholders come together and reflect on the destination goals (Koens et al. 2020).

The value added of the augmented blueprint in collaborative design lies in the ability to map tourist experience based on strategic visitor flows, to identify the relevant stakeholders able to attract the flows, to assign the responsibilities and stimulate cooperation. The higher willingness to cooperate and the assignment of responsibilities ensure that the governance of a destination will be efficient and can be controlled (Figure 7.1).

However, as noted by Beritelli (2019), visitors who stay for a longer period in a destination engage in different activities and, therefore, participate in different flows. The diversity and interconnectivity of flows allow destination stakeholders to take part in co-creating experiences for tourists in the areas visited by these flows. At the forefront is the ability of stakeholders to address and manage the identified visitor flows and create a synergic effect for the entire portfolio of flows. In order to ensure the long-term success of a destination and from the global point of view, it is worth also taking into account that the more diverse the flows in a destination are, the more likely the whole destination will have all-year-round visitation. As each stakeholder possesses only limited information on specific visitor flow that is able to reach, the knowledge transfer among stakeholders is needed. In order to create the synergic effect for the entire portfolio of flows, stakeholders should possess, share relevant information and produce knowledge. Therefore, dynamic knowledge exchange among stakeholders can help to govern the destination in a smart way.

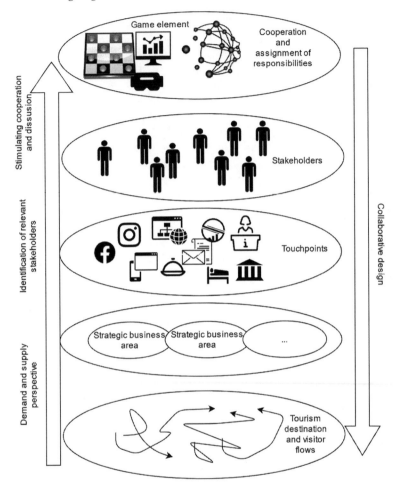

Figure 7.1 Augmented service blueprint strengthening collaborative design.

7.2 Knowledge sharing through intelligent information system

The knowledge management perspective requires investments in smart solutions in order to take advantage of the massive amount of available data and implement the policy of open data to stimulate entrepreneurial ventures (Vargas 2020). Moreover, based on the analysis of the role of a DMO in the smart tourism ecosystem, the DMO should be the leader of knowledge transfer. Successful DMO of the future should be an intelligent agent that is able to identify, engage and learn from diverse internal and external stakeholders by acquiring, filtering and analysing data from various sources in order to create sufficient knowledge (Sheehan et al. 2016).

The development of Internet technologies and the increased use of electronic platforms by tourists push forward the creation of an intelligent destination information system that facilitates exploitation of smart data and their transformation to knowledge, inevitable for smart destination governance. Despite the recognised need for an information system for a smart tourism destination, there has been little attempt to conceptualise the requirements into one model. Therefore, conceptualising the model of intelligent information systems can strengthen the theory and practice of smart destination governance. Intelligent systems encompass technologies that can sense the environment and learn from data they receive in response to their actions (Gretzel 2011). The conceptual model is based on state-of-the-art technologies focusing on their connection and contribution to smart destination concept. The intelligent information system for smart destination governance should contain three layers focusing on collecting data, their processing and exchange (Figure 7.2).

The effectiveness of knowledge transfer in the intelligent information system is empowered by real-time monitoring using the Internet of Things (IoT). However, not all data can be collected in real time, therefore intelligent information system uses online and offline data processing. Moreover, thanks to the benefits facilitated by cloud computing, the architecture of the system is a cloud-based platform. It enables storage and access to data and seamless integration of components and layers. The use of AI helps to process the data and make recommendations (Figure 7.3).

The *data collection layer* of the intelligent information system is composed of personal, behavioural, geographical and other data from different sources and owners. Google, a giant search engine in Europe, collects its own dynamic data on Internet searches, IDS/OTA providers have their own booking and searching databases, mobile operators store their own location data and also destination stakeholders (e.g. hotels) use their own eCRM databases. Moreover, the sensors embedded in destinations environment have many times their own owners (e.g. DMO, retail shops, police). To obtain the data from these owners, direct links through APIs should be used to support the real-time transfer.

The personal data contain the name, age and gender of tourists obtained from social media (social networks, blogs, media-related sites), mobile apps and destination smart cards. Moreover, it comprises the booking ID (or newsletter subscriber ID) of a tourist from IDS/OTA, destination websites and DMS.

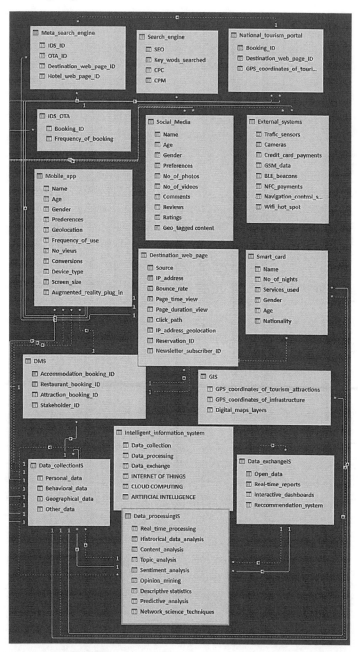

Figure 7.2 Architecture of intelligent information system for tourism destinations.

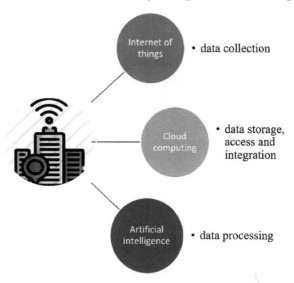

Internet of things   • data collection

Cloud computing   • data storage, access and integration

Artificial intelligence   • data processing

Figure 7.3 The use of state-of-the-art technologies in intelligent information systems.

The behavioural data are of quantitative and qualitative matter. The sources of quantitative data are websites, mobile app analytics or external systems. These can include bounce rate, page time view, page duration view and click path from destination website, frequency of use, as well as the number of users of a mobile app. Traffic sensors and cameras can provide information on the number of vehicles or the overcrowding of tourist attractions. Information about tourist consumption in a destination can be derived from credit card payments or payments via NFC. Social media provide mainly qualitative information on preferences, comments and reviews made by tourists. These data are valuable for the smart destination governance concept, as they allow the personalisation of experiences and enable steering the tourist behaviour.

Geographic data give information on tourist origins, such as IP address geolocation, or tourist movement, thanks to active location-based services in a smartphone launched by a mobile app, or passive mobile positioning via GSM data obtained from mobile operators. Moreover, Bluetooth low energy in beacons, used mainly inside tourist attractions, can provide useful information about visitor flows inside a building. GPS coordinates of tourist attractions and infrastructure, as well as digital map layers from desktop and online GIS, are also important sources of geographic data for further analysis.

The *data processing layer* is based on real-time processing of all collected data. This data is of different format (structured, semi-structured, unstructured) and require different techniques for extraction. The unstructured data (e.g. images, videos, reviews) are proceeded by content analysis. Within the content analysis, topic analysis uses text mining to detect and understand the language and image analysis for object detection. Opinion mining and sentiment analysis based on supervised and unsupervised methods are used to analyse opinions and sentiments of comments and reviews. Structured data are processed by structure analysis. Concerning the structure analysis, the size, heterogeneous nature and complexity of data put pressure on the automatic treatment and analysis. The applicability of traditional statistical methods for real time and big data is questioned due to statistical insignificance in large datasets or false positive correlation. Therefore, traditional methods should be enriched with new ones to contribute to smart destination governance. Besides descriptive analytics (e.g. sum, averages, percentages) and predictive analytics (e.g. autoregressive integrated moving average – ARIMA), the system also uses prescriptive analytics enhanced by artificial intelligence. Moreover, based on the analysis of the applicability of network science techniques to large-scale data, network analysis is used to measure relationships in a destination, support the time series and mobility analysis.

The application of business intelligence allows to create sufficient knowledge in a destination. Within business intelligence, data mining using machine learning, statistics and modelling enables to discover unknown patterns in data and handle complex unstructured data from multiple data sources in order to turn this data into actionable strategies for better decision-making. Except for actual data, the database of intelligent information system contains also historical data in order to apply the revenue management concept and forecast demand, as well as apply dynamic pricing. The geo-localised data allows the identification of visitor flows and therefore to identify the zones dedicated to tourism and density of tourists. The cross-referencing of all data provides an automatic classification of destination zones, tourist typologies and customer relationship management leading to the provision of highly personalised experience and thus contributing to experience design.

The *data exchange layer* is composed of open data, in order to stimulate information sharing between tourism stakeholders. All collected and processed data are available in real time and support the 'soft smartness' of a destination. The intelligent information system provides interactive dashboards for managers and stakeholders leading to the provision of real-time reports. These reports enable more effective and efficient destination governance as well as they contribute to the management of stakeholders' businesses. The recommendation system allows to perform right decisions, while the marketing system automatically sends newsletters and push notifications to tourists and uses the channel manager to adjust availability and prices of bookings. The data exchange layer uses open data for stimulation of knowledge diffusion and provides real-time dashboards for destination stakeholders, which creates opportunities for co-decision.

The use of this system bridges the challenge of unused data in a destination (Fuchs et al. 2014) and provides opportunities to take knowledge from information proceeded and data collected (Figure 7.4).

In this sense, knowledge has become a critical requirement of smart destination governance, where knowing the current performance of a destination and the behaviour of tourists can significantly affect the success of a destination (Choe & Fesenmaier 2021). The proposed model of intelligent information system is able to create sufficient knowledge for better decisions by collecting, integrating and analysing available data.

7.3 Smart solutions enhancing sustainability, competitiveness and resilience

Summarising the results of the presented research, the smart approach provides opportunities for more sustainable governance of a destination, can lead to higher competitiveness, and is able to positively influence the resilience of a destination. The ability to collect, monitor, analyse and visualise data from various sources in real time allows effective and timely decisions. The biggest opportunity is to use the knowledge to change tourist behaviour. More transparent information about the destination, its services and capacities, available in real time, can be combined with intelligent recommendations using recommender systems that can provide more sustainable alternatives to encourage behavioural changes. Moreover, smart solutions can provide numerous incentives for choosing the more sustainable alternative using the reward systems, real-time benefits or by providing transparent information, raising awareness or nudging (Schmücker et al. 2019).

As the intelligent information system allows linking different datasets from various stakeholders, it follows the principal mechanism that connects smartness with sustainability. It is the ability to collect and measure indicators of sustainable development and support

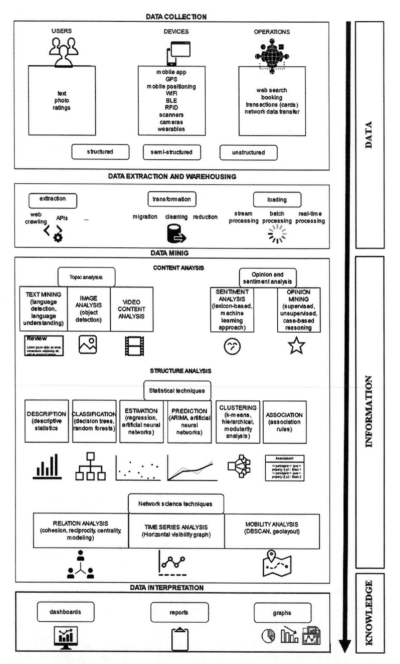

Figure 7.4 From data to information and knowledge in a destination.

decision-making processes and communication with stakeholders (Perles Ribes & Ivars Baidal 2018). Adopting the triple-bottom-line accounting by accessing the economic, social and environmental dimensions, can lead to the achievement of sustainable development goals in tourism destinations and can address the often overlooked sustainability in the smart tourism concept (Table 7.3).

Different data sources allow accessing different dimensions of sustainability. Data on tourists and their behaviour contributes to the economic dimension and can be used to deal with issues relating to carrying capacities and overtourism. Visitor flows, consumption of resources and activities of tourists can be measured more easily and resource-saving measures can be adopted based on available data (Schmücker et al. 2019). The social dimension is easily accessed by data from social media and DMS representing the host–guest relationship and tourist satisfaction. The connection between sensors and GIS allows studying environmental issues in a destination.

The knowledge of sustainability indicators can translate into more efficient use of resources, better-quality life, experience enrichment and environmental sustainability. Managers do not need to wait months or years to calculate sustainability indicators; however, the warning system based on big data analytics can provide alerts and recommendations to ensure the sustainability of a destination.

Knowledge sharing also facilitates better governance processes; strengthen public–private cooperation and increases transparency. Considering the strengthening of collaborative design, the ability to identify the position of stakeholders in a destination and stimulate the

Table 7.3 Using smart approach to address sustainability issues in a destination

Sustainable Pillar	Indicator	Means of Collection
Economic	Number and flow of tourists	Mobile positioning, smart cards, scanners, mobile app
	Tourists' spending	Bank cards
	Rise of prices	External web sites
Social	Criminality	Cameras
	Atmosphere	Social media
	Satisfaction of tourists	Social media
	Cooperation in a destination	DMS
Environmental	Air cleanliness	Air sensors
	Transport situation	Traffic sensors, cameras
	Landscape look	Wearables, social media, GIS

cooperation leads to higher competitiveness. Augmented service blue-printing can help stakeholders to consider more the role of technology in tourist journey and to overcome the barriers of cooperation in a destination. As the competitiveness of a destination lies in the ability to link the stakeholders dynamically, knowledge sharing within the smart approach creates several opportunities for data exchange and simulations. Based on the size of data transfer, the amount of information exchanged can be measured, providing useful managerial outcomes.

Destination resilience is influenced by the ability to make decisions based on collective information, and thus create strategies that reduce the vulnerability of a destination and increase its flexibility. The precise modelling of a destination ecosystem, taking into account the diffusion of knowledge, can be applied to build more resilient destinations. The smart approach enables to use more complex and real-time data and includes a wider variety of information about stakeholders (e.g. the probability of willingness to share information with cooperating neighbours and the probability to stop the information measured by the actual size of data exchange) (Figure 7.5). This also overcomes the limitations of today's research (e.g. Baggio, Micera, & Del Chiappa 2020), where the absorptive capacity, presenting the ability to acquire, retain and transfer the knowledge, has been so far arbitrary assigned.

```
#Model building
def diffusion_model_of_knowledge_sharing| (pShare, pStop)
  def model (g,i):
  #if a stakeholder have an information
  if g.node[i]['state']== INFO
    # share information with cooperating stakeholders with probability pShare
    for m in g.neighbors(i):
      if g.node[m]['state']==SHARE
        if rnd.random()<= pShare
          g.node[m]['state']==INFO
          #stop sharing with probability Stop
          if rnd.random()<=pStop
            g.node[i]['state']==STOP
  return model

#One step
def diffusion_step(g, model):
  for i in g.node.keys():
    model (g,i)
  #count states and add to step
  info = cnt_state(g, INFO)
  stop = cnt_state(g,STOP)
  share = cnt_state(g, SHARE)
  INF.append(info)
  SH.append(share)
  STO.append(stop)

#Run N iteration
def diffusion_run(g, mdl, N):
  for i in range(N):
    diffusion_step(g, mdl)
```

Figure 7.5 Example of diffusion model of knowledge sharing in a destination.

Therefore, it can be concluded that applying the design-based perspectives for smart destination governance can lead to more competitive, sustainable and resilient destination development.

References

Baggio, R., and Cooper, C., 2010. Knowledge transfer in a tourism destination: The effects of a network structure. *Service Industries Journal*, 30 (10), 1757–1771.

Baggio, R., Micera, R., and Del Chiappa, G., 2020. Smart tourism destinations: A critical reflection. *Journal of Hospitality and Tourism Technology*, 11 (3), 407–423.

Beritelli, P., 2019. Transferring concepts and tools from other fields to the tourist destination: A critical viewpoint focusing on the lifecycle concept. *Journal of Destination Marketing and Management*, 14 (December 2019), 100384.

Beritelli, P., Laesser, C., Reinhold, S., and Kappler, A., 2013. *Das St. Galler modell fur destinationsmanagement: Geschäftsmodellinnovation in netzwerken*. St. Gallen: IMP-HSF.

Beritelli, P., Reinhold, S., and Laesser, C., 2020. Visitor flows, trajectories and corridors: Planning and designing places from the traveler's point of view. *Annals of Tourism Research*, 82 (April), 102936.

Buhalis, D., and Amaranggana, A., 2015. Smart tourism destinations enhancing tourism experience through personalisation of services. *In*: I. Tussyadiah, and A. Inversini, eds. *Information and communication technologies in tourism 2015*. Cham: Springer International Publishing Switzerland, 377–389.

Buonincontri, P., and Micera, R., 2016. The experience co-creation in smart tourism destinations: A multiple case analysis of European destinations. *Information Technology and Tourism*, 16 (3), 285–315.

Choe, Y., and Fesenmaier, D.R., 2021. Designing an advanced system for destination management: A case study of Northern Indiana. *Industrial Management and Data Systems*, 121 (6), 1167–1190.

Cizel, B., Ajanovic, E., and Cakar, K., 2016. Prerequisites for effective and sustainable destination governance. *Anatolia*, 27 (2), 155–166.

Eichelberger, S., Peters, M., Pikkemaat, B., and Chan, C.S., 2020. Entrepreneurial ecosystems in smart cities for tourism development: From stakeholder perceptions to regional tourism policy implications. *Journal of Hospitality and Tourism Management*, 45, 319–329.

Fuchs, M., Höpken, W., and Lexhagen, M., 2014. Big data analytics for knowledge generation in tourism destinations – A case from Sweden. *Journal of Destination Marketing & Management*, 3 (4), 198–209.

Gretzel, U., 2011. Intelligent systems in tourism: A social science perspective. *Annals of Tourism Research*, 38 (3), 757–779.

Gretzel, U., Sigala, M., Xiang, Z., and Koo, C., 2015. Smart tourism: Foundations and developments. *Electronic Markets*, 25 (3), 179–188.

Koens, K., Klijs, J., Weber-Sabil, J., Melissen, F., Lalicic, L., Mayer, I., Önder, I., and Aall, C., 2020. Serious gaming to stimulate participatory urban tourism planning. *Journal of Sustainable Tourism*, 1–20.

Park, S., Xu, Y., Jiang, L., Chen, Z., and Huang, S., 2020. Spatial structures of tourism destinations: A trajectory data mining approach leveraging mobile big data. *Annals of Tourism Research*, 84 (January), 102973.

Pereira, G.V., Parycek, P., Falco, E., and Kleinhans, R., 2018. Smart governance in the context of smart cities: A literature review. *Information Polity*, 23 (2), 143–162.

Perles Ribes, J.F., and Ivars Baidal, J., 2018. Smart sustainability: A new perspective in the sustainable tourism debate. *Investigaciones Regionales*, 42 (1), 151–170.

Schmücker, D., Horster, E., and Kreilkamp, E., 2019. *The impact of digitisation and big data analysis on the sustainable developemnt of tourism and its environmental impact*. Dessau-Rosslau: Umweltbundesamt.

Sheehan, L., Vargas-Sánchez, A., Presenza, A., and Abbate, T., 2016. The use of intelligence in tourism destination management: An emerging role for DMOs. *International Journal of Tourism Research*, 18 (6), 549–557.

Vargas, A., 2020. Covid-19 crisis: A new model of tourism governance for a new time. *Worldwide Hospitality and Tourism Themes*, 12 (6), 691–699.

Conclusion

Smart tourism destination governance has the ability to be the key factor for the success of tourism destinations. It supports the sustainability, competitiveness and resilience of tourism destinations. This approach to tourism destination development is suitable for mature destinations that have the resources and time to focus on technology and design principles. So far, the contribution of smart governance to destination development has been examined mainly from a conceptual point of view. This book is one of the first to address this phenomenon empirically.

Smart tourism destination governance pushes forward the decision-making based on available data and encompasses the network of all relevant stakeholders. Data are seen as a 'new oil' and smart governance as a new concept improving decision-making processes, stimulating the design of tourist experience and collaborative design through smart solutions, and thus propelling destination sustainability, competitiveness and resilience. Although the presented opportunities of the smart approach to destination governance provide useful strategies for mature destinations with powerful and real-time impact, in practice, it is still difficult for destinations to engage in these practices due to the lack of financial, technical and human resources. However, smart tourism initiatives are financially supported by many national and international policies. Therefore, in the near future, we can expect the rise of smart governance in the praxis of many destinations.

Although the presented research has made an important contribution to smart destination development, it has several limitations. These limitations lie in the analysis of destination governance in one country, which is considered a digital challenger. Although this approach enables to consider real conditions and problems of destination governance many destinations in the world have to face, the data availability was in some cases limited. Moreover, biases of the questionnaire

DOI: 10.4324/9781003269342-12

survey (e.g. belief vs. behaviour) could also have influenced the outcomes. Therefore, there are several implications for further research. Firstly, the situation in other destinations and countries could bring more light to the phenomenon of smart destination governance. More quantitative and qualitative studies can extend the research findings.

Studies focusing on quantitative approach can use data from mobile apps, sensors, search engines (e.g. Google Trends), cards or wearables to compare the findings. New qualitative research approaches can help to deeply analyse the phenomenon. Using collaborative visual ethnography, researchers and participants (tourists, local community) can work together to identify, explore and share thoughts on problems through images and videos. These visuals can be further analysed and composite images can be built as prototypes to represent the analysed phenomena. This method is capable of analysing and supporting creative problem solving, therefore, it is ideal for smart tourism destination research. Moreover, the application of network analysis can be extended by visual network analysis, focusing on the visualisation and interpretation of qualitative data by means of network diagrams. Moreover, it should be taken into account that future developments will blur the boundaries between the physical world and the virtual world, creating new perspectives for smart destination governance.

The outcomes of the research are valuable for scholars focusing on destination governance, smart tourism development or destination design. They can find here the methodological guidelines as well as inspiration for their further research. Decision-makers in tourism destinations can find inspiration on how to strengthen the governance of their destination and make the destination more competitive, sustainable and resilient.

Index

Page numbers in **bold** indicate tables, page numbers in *italic* indicate figures

For Product Safety Concerns and Information please contact our EU
representative GPSR@taylorandfrancis.com Taylor & Francis Verlag GmbH,
Kaufingerstraße 24, 80331 München, Germany

Printed and bound by CPI Group (UK) Ltd, Croydon, CR0 4YY
11/04/2025
01844010-0018